Designing Netware Directory Services™

Designing NetWare Directory Services™

Gamal Herbon

M&T Books
A Division of MIS:Press
A Subsidiary of Henry Holt and Company, Inc.
115 West 18th Street
New York, New York 10011

Library of Congress Cataloging–in–Publication Data

```
Herbon, Gamal B.
    Designing NetWare directory services/Gamal B. Herbon.
       p. cm.
    Includes index.
    ISBN 1-55851-338-8 : $29.95
    1. NetWare (Computer file) 2. Local area networks (Computer networks)
    I. Title
    TK5105.7.H47  1994                          94-1548
    005.7'1369--dc20                            CIP
```

Publisher: Steve Berkowitz
Associate Publisher: Brenda McLaughlin
Project Editor: Jules Gilder
Development Editor: Ken Neff
Production Editor: Mark Masuelli
Associate Production Editor: Joseph McPartland
Illustrations: Joseph McPartland, Maya Riddick
Copy Editor: Dawn Erdos
Technical Editor: Ken Neff

97   96   95   94   4   3   2   1

Table of Contents

Section 11: Implementing

Section 111: Maintaining

Section IV: Appendices

Acknowledgments

Many thanks go to the following people:

Edward Liebing, my friend and the person responsible for the creation of this book.

Warren Harding, Robb Perry and the Novell Systems Research department for encouragement and technical help, as well as for their permission to use information from the *NetWare Application Notes*.

To Novell for producing the NetWare 4 operating system and NetWare Directory Services.

To Cheryl Goldberg and Jules Gilder for all of their efforts in putting this book together. To all others who have helped me during this endeavor (you know who you are).

To my wife, Terilee, our children Justin, Kristin, and Leann, and the many other family members who have been patient and encouraging throughout this process.

And finally, to my good friend and editor, Ken Neff, for his hard work, steady encouragement, and guidance, and for his friendship, which made this book happen.

Why This Book is for You

Designing, installing, and managing a NetWare 4 network is a challenge even for the most knowledgeable network administrator. The most important new aspect of Novell's powerful enterprise networking software is the addition of NetWare Directory Services™ (NDS). *Designing NetWare Directory Services* is a valuable resource to help you take advantage of the enhanced features NDS provides. It contains a wealth of detailed information about how NDS works, what benefits it offers, and how to plan for and implement a successful installation. Throughout this book, you'll find practical suggestions for Directory tree planning, simple guidelines for installing Directory Services in NetWare 4, advice on how to manage NDS once it is installed, and tips for avoiding common pitfalls along the way.

Newcomers to NetWare 4 and seasoned NetWare veterans alike will benefit from this book's technical overview and conceptual discussions. This material is intended to provide the insights necessary to understand and work more confidently with the interrelated components of NDS. The planning, installation, and management sections of this book are designed to appeal to a wide range of audiences:

1

- If you are a NetWare designer, consultant, or installer, you'll find practical advice on how to properly plan for and install Directory Services on NetWare 4 servers. You'll also see what is involved in installing the new DOS/Windows client software on workstations. You can use this book as a research tool in planning an effective NDS implementation.

- If you are a network administrator or MIS staff member, you'll find useful suggestions for setting up the Directory tree, setting up NDS security, managing partitions and replicas, configuring time synchronization, and providing bindery emulation. You'll also find the management section of the book helpful in dealing with the day-to-day maintenance of the Directory.

- If you are a NetWare service technician or support provider, you can use the troubleshooting information to enhance your knowledge base and raise your level of expertise in isolating and fixing NDS problems.

As a reference focused exclusively on working with Directory Services, *Designing NetWare Directory Services* is an indispensable tool for anyone charged with designing and implementing a high-end NetWare 4 network.

Section 1

Planning for NetWare Directory Services

Introduction to NetWare Directory Services

NetWare 4 is the most advanced network operating system ever introduced by Novell. With NetWare 4, the network transcends the confines of the departmental LAN and enters the realm of the "enterprise," or global, network. At the center of this new enterprise network paradigm, and at the heart of NetWare 4, is NetWare Directory Services.

NetWare Directory Services™ (NDS) allows you to integrate a highly diverse collection of network resources into a cohesive computing environment. It provides global naming services, enhanced network security, and easy network management.

This chapter introduces the basic concepts behind NetWare Directory Services and related services in NetWare 4. It provides an overview of such topics as Directory objects and properties, the Directory tree structure, NDS security and administration, partitions and replicas, network time synchronization, and bindery emulation.

NetWare Directory Services Overview

What is NetWare Directory Services? How can NDS improve my network or make it easier to manage? These are questions network administrators and system integrators have been asking since the release of NetWare 4.0. To answer these questions, I'll start with a "textbook" definition.

> *NetWare Directory Services*: a globally distributed, replicated, loosely consistent database, based in part on the International Telephone and Telegraph Consultive Committee's (CCITT) proposed X.500 standards. The NDS database maintains information about and controls access to all network resources. NDS allows users to login once to the network and thereby gain access to all services and resources they have rights to use.

Now let's examine each aspect of this NetWare Directory Services definition a little more closely.

Global database

First and foremost, NetWare Directory Services is a global database of network resources. The NDS database maintains information about all network resources, including (but not limited to) users, groups, servers, volumes, print queues, printers, and modems. The name *Directory* comes from the name commonly used for telephone books. It has nothing to do with the directory structure used in NetWare's file system.

NDS maintains the network resource information in a hierarchical tree structure; hence the name *Directory tree*. This structure allows network resources to be organized in the tree independent of their physical location on the network. Network users can then access network resources they have proper rights to, without always having to know the exact location of the resource they want to use.

In previous versions of NetWare (2 and 3), the NetWare *bindery* is the system database that stores information about network resources on a server-by-server basis. In NetWare 4, the NDS database replaces the bindery. Rather than being single-server centric as the bindery is, the NDS database supports an entire network of servers. The global nature of NDS allows greater management flexibility as well as easier access to the resources users need.

It should be noted here that although NetWare 4 leaves the bindery behind in favor of NDS, it is backward compatible with bindery-based versions of NetWare through the bindery emulation feature.

Distributed and replicated

Unlike the bindery, which exists on each NetWare server and maintains information about just that server and its resources, the NDS database is distributed around the network and maintains information about all network servers and resources. No matter where servers and users are physically located, they can easily access information anywhere on the network (provided they have been granted access, of course).

On large networks, it would be impractical to distribute the entire database onto every server. Thus NetWare 4 allows the Directory's global database to be divided into logical portions called *partitions*. An NDS partition is a distinct unit of data used to store information about a portion of the Directory. A partition can be thought of as a single branch or subtree within the Directory tree.

These partitions can and should be replicated. *Replicas* are copies of NDS partitions kept on various servers around the network. They have two main purposes:

1. to provide for Directory fault tolerance by eliminating the risk of any single point of failure for the Directory—a crucial factor in enterprise networks.

2. to allow for faster access to Directory information across WAN links.

Loosely consistent

One of the challenges in maintaining a globally distributed database is keeping all of the information up to date when changes are made. For example, when you create a new user in a partition, the change must be propagated to all replicas of that partition. With NDS, this synchronization between replicas happens automatically in the background. No user intervention is necessary.

The term *loosely consistent* means the NDS database is not necessarily in strict synchronization all of the time. When major changes are made the Directory, such as moving a server or joining two partitions, it can take a while for the changes to propagate to all replicas. Thus, there can be periods of time during which the information in one replica is different from that in another replica. But the replicas do eventually converge to an identical state, making the Directory consistent once again.

Based on X.500 standards

In designing NetWare Directory Services, Novell based its implementation on parts of the X.500 Directory Recommendations proposed by the International Telephone and Telegraph Consultative Committee (CCITT) and the International Standards Organization (ISO). These standards were first published in 1988, but have since been revised. As of this writing, the 1992 version is still waiting to be approved.

Some people question why Novell did not adhere strictly to the X.500 standard when designing the NDS Directory. There are several reasons. First, at the time NetWare 4 was being developed, the standard was still in the proposal stage. The NDS engineers knew that many aspects of this early version were likely to change before the standard could be approved. Second, they wanted to add important enhancements such as access control, which was not included in the 1988 guidelines. By not locking NDS into the X.500 standard that had yet to be approved, NetWare 4 allows for future expansion of the Directory and the possible services it can provide.

On the other hand, the NetWare 4 Directory is based on enough of the X.500 recommendations as to allow NDS-based systems to interoperate in some fashion with other X.500-based directories. Even though each vendor's X.500 implementation may be slightly different, the basic architectures should be similar enough so they can be connected through some type of gateway. This interoperability will make it possible to exchange information with other name services across multiple organizations. Such cross-company Directory capabilities will become increasingly important in the global marketplace of the future.

Network login

Since NDS is a globally distributed and replicated database, it is possible for users to login to the entire network, rather than login to a specific server. In NetWare versions 2 and 3, users must specify the name of the server to which they want to attach. For example, user THERBON would login to server FS1 by typing:

```
LOGIN FS1/THERBON
```

In NetWare 4, you can still login directly to a NetWare server, but it is no longer necessary to do so to access network resources and services. To login to the network, all user THERBON has to do is type:

```
LOGIN THERBON
```

This type of login is possible because multiple copies (replicas) of each user's required login information are spread throughout the network, usually on several servers. Users can login to the network even if their "home" or primary server is down, provided any server that holds a copy of the necessary login information is operational. While users cannot access services that reside on a server that is off-line, they can still login and access all other services and resources for which they have proper access rights.

With a single network login, users can access network resources or services without having to explicitly login or attach to each and every server on which those resources or services reside. Once they have been identified and authenticated on the network, users automatically are attached to any necessary servers that provide the services they have rights to access. This is what is meant by servers being *transparent* to the process of using the network.

NDS handles the authentication process and all name-to-address mapping in the background, without the user being aware of what is going on. This shields users from the complexity of having to understand or deal with network topology, protocols, communication links, or media, thus making the network easier to use.

Authentication and access control

Whenever a user accesses network resources (such as servers, volumes, and printers), authentication occurs in the background. This authentication process verifies whether the requesting user has sufficient rights to use the requested resource.

The network-wide login and background authentication provided by NDS locks out unauthorized users. At the same time, it is easier for authorized users to use the network and access resources. Users need only one password to gain access to all network resources for which they have the proper rights. In NetWare 4, a separate set of NDS rights is used to allow or restrict access to the Directory database.

Separate from the NetWare file system

While NDS provides for easier network and resource management, it is important to understand that NDS does *not* directly control the NetWare file system. Volumes, file system directories, and files are managed by NetWare 4 utilities that are available in both text-based and graphical user interface (GUI) versions. Thus, it is possible to have separate administrators for NDS and for the file system. In large networks, or for security reasons, such a division of responsibility may be preferable.

A new networking paradigm

NetWare Directory Services introduces some powerful new technologies and capabilities for networks. Those who are familiar with previous versions of NetWare will need to change the way they think about networking and how users access network services and resources. Users no longer have to login to a specific server and expect that server to provide all network services and access to all necessary resources. Instead, users login to the network and may access services and resources without having to know where on the network those services or resources reside.

In addition to making the network easier to use, NDS also allows for enhanced network security and easier network management. Formerly, a user had to be defined and granted appropriate rights on every server the user needed to access (home file server, e-mail server, database server, and so on). Several user accounts had to be maintained for the same person, and that person had to remember numerous passwords and know the exact location of any resource or server he or she needed to access. On large networks with many users, this can become quite labor intensive.

In the brave new world of NetWare 4 and NDS, a user is defined only once on the network. The administrator then only has to deal with one user account when setting up access rights to all necessary resources, services, and applications.

To derive the most benefit from NetWare Directory Services, you need to start viewing the network as a single, unified system, rather than as a fragmented collection of computers, printers, and other resources. While this change in mindset may take some getting used to, the payoff is great, both for the network administrator and for the users.

With NDS, NetWare 4 brings PCs into the enterprise network arena as a viable alternative to minicomputers and mainframe systems. Capabilities such as centralized administration and advanced security, which have endeared many MIS departments to minicomputers and mainframes, are now available much less expensively in NetWare.

The NDS Directory Tree

The Directory tree—the hierarchical structure of the NDS database—is formed by placing network *objects* into this hierarchy. NDS objects include categories of information known as *properties,* along with their associated values. All object and property information is stored in the Directory database.

NDS objects and properties

NDS objects are not physical items (such as printers or servers). Rather, they are structures that store information about the entities or resources they represent. For example, a server object stores information about a specific server and helps manage how the server is used—but it is not the physical server itself.

For each type of NDS object, categories of information—properties—are defined. Properties contain information specific to that particular object. Different types of NDS objects have different properties. While one type of NDS object might have only three properties, another might have 10 or more. The number of properties depends on the amount of information defined in the *schema* for each object. Some object properties are mandatory (they must contain information for the object to be a valid NDS object), while others are optional (they can contain information if desired, but it is not required).

How NDS objects form the Directory tree

The location of objects in the tree determines the structure and function of the different branches of the Directory tree, as well as the Directory structure as a whole. Using time-honored computer-science convention, this tree structure has the tree growing upside down with the "root" object at the top of the tree and the other objects branching downward from there.

The NDS Directory tree is made up of three types of objects:

1. The [Root] object (always referred to with square brackets surrounding the word Root)

2. Container objects

3. Leaf objects

Since every tree must have roots, the NetWare 4 installation program automatically places the [*Root*] object at the top of the Directory tree. This mandatory object cannot be renamed or deleted.

The various branches of the Directory tree are made up of *container* objects. Container objects can hold (or contain) other objects—even other container objects. Container objects provide a means of logically organizing all other objects in the Directory tree. In the Directory, container objects are used similar to the way directories are used in the file system. Where file system directories group related files together in a file system, container objects group related items in the Directory tree.

NDS *leaf* objects are so named because they are located at the ends of the branches in the Directory tree. Leaf objects cannot contain any other objects. They represent actual network entities such as users, servers, printers, and computers.

NetWare Directory Services allows you the flexibility to place container objects and leaf objects in various tree configurations, according to what best suits the needs of your company or organization. Some may choose a wide, flat tree structure with few levels of containers. Others may need a narrower, deeper tree structure. It is important to realize at the outset that there is no one "right way" to design or implement your Directory tree. The information in this book will help you choose the best implementation of the Directory for your specific needs.

Chapter 2 discusses in more detail NDS objects, properties, and how they form the Directory tree structure.

NDS Security and Administration

To control access to network information, NetWare 4 provides four different sets of rights:

1. File system directory rights

2. File system file rights

3. NDS object rights

4. NDS property rights

The NetWare file system has slightly different sets of rights for directories and for files. These are entirely separate from the NDS object and property rights, and therefore will not be covered in this book. In a similar manner, however, NDS provides separate sets of rights for objects and for properties.

Object and property rights

NDS object and property rights determine what you can and can't do within the Directory. Object and property rights are assigned separately to provide enhanced security and better network access control to the information (properties) contained in NDS objects.

As is typical in a hierarchical tree structure such as NDS, rights assigned in the upper levels of the Directory flow down through the tree. This is an important concept to understand when designing a Directory tree of any size.

Creating and managing objects

Some of the most important tasks you will perform in NetWare 4 involve creating and managing NDS objects. Novell provides two new administration utilities for creating and managing NDS objects: NETADMIN (a text-based utility) and NWAdmin (a graphical utility). Both utilities do essentially the same things—the choice of which one to use is yours. I discuss how to use these utilities in various chapters throughout this book.

When you first install a NetWare 4 server, a user object named Admin is automatically created and given all rights to every object and property in the Directory tree. This is the object the network administrator or supervisor will use to login to the network and set up the other objects in the tree.

In this respect, user Admin is analogous to SUPERVISOR in previous versions of NetWare. However, in NetWare 4 user Admin is not granted any special status—it is an object just like any other. Admin is assigned all rights simply because it is the first object created in the Directory. Its rights can be blocked in lower portions of the tree, and it can even be deleted (although you need to be careful when doing either of these things).

Chapter 3 provides more detail about object and property rights, NDS access control, and user Admin.

NDS Partitions and Replicas

NDS partitions are logical divisions (or portions) of the Directory's global database. Replicas are copies of NDS partitions that can be distributed to various servers around the network. By properly setting up and managing partitions and replicas, you can provide fault tolerance for the Directory database by eliminating any single point of failure. You can also allow for faster access to Directory information across WAN links.

As your organization changes and grows, you may find it necessary to split or merge partitions in the Directory tree. Novell provides two utilities for performing this type of partition and replica management: PARTMGR (a text-based utility) and the Partition Manager tool (a graphical utility). Again, the choice of which version to use is yours.

Chapter 4 contains more information about NDS partitions and replicas.

Network Time Synchronization

NetWare Directory Services requires a new NetWare 4 feature known as *time synchronization*. Servers on the network can be designated to act as "time source" servers. Other servers can then synchronize their clocks with these time sources to keep the network's time consistent, even across time zones or across continents. Time synchronization services are used to establish the chronological order in which Directory events take place, so that servers receiving updates to their replicas can tell which is the latest information.

In the rare case when two (or more) conflicting changes are made to the same object at the same time, only the one with the latest modification timestamp will be made. NDS relies on network-wide time synchronization to determine the latest modification.

Chapter 5 discusses time synchronization and how to set up time source servers on your network.

NetWare Bindery Compatibility

Because of the large installed base of NetWare 2 and 3 networks, Novell offers *bindery emulation* in NetWare 4 to provide backward compatibility with these bindery-based operating systems. In many cases it is not practical to upgrade all existing servers to NetWare 4 at once. Bindery emulation allows "mixed" networks to coexist until customers decide to move all of their servers to the NetWare 4 platform.

Bindery emulation allows bindery-based NetWare utilities, NetWare Loadable Modules (NLMs), and client software to coexist with NDS. When properly set up for bindery emulation, NDS imitates a flat bindery-type structure for leaf objects in a particular container. Thus, with bindery emulation enabled, all objects in the specified container can be accessed by both NDS objects and bindery-based servers and clients. Bindery emulation applies only to leaf objects in the specified container object where bindery emulation is enabled.

Chapter 6 gives more information about bindery emulation, its uses, and limitations.

Summary

This chapter has introduced the basic concepts necessary to understand what NetWare Directory Services is, what NDS can offer in a NetWare 4 network, and what is involved in creating and managing a Directory tree.

Subsequent chapters explain these concepts in more detail. These planning chapters provide guidelines for designing and configuring NetWare 4 Directory trees to meet various needs. They also include suggestions for configuring and optimizing your network through the use of NDS. Finally, they present several examples of Directory Services implementations so you can see how the theory can be applied to real-world situations.

The Directory Tree

Understanding the Directory tree and how it works is critical to designing a successful NetWare 4 network. This chapter presents an in-depth look at the various types of objects that form the NDS Directory tree, along with some simple configuration examples. It explains more about contexts and object names, and gives some tips for establishing NDS object naming conventions.

Types of NDS Objects

The structure of the NDS database, or Directory tree, is formed by placing network objects in a hierarchical structure. The different types of objects that form the NDS database can be categorized as follows:

- Physical objects (representing users, printers, servers, modems, and so on)

- Logical objects (representing groups, print queues, and so on)

- Other objects (such as Organizational Units) designed to organize and manage physical and logical objects

Remember that NDS objects are data structures that store information, not the actual entity represented by the object. For example, a Printer object stores information about a specific printer and helps manage how the printer is used, but it is not the physical printer itself.

Every NDS object has certain properties that contain specific information about that object. NDS properties are categories of information that are stored in the NDS database for all objects. For a user, the information in these properties might include the user's telephone number and address. For a printer, it might include the printer's physical location.

Each NDS object has specific information, or values, that are entered into data fields for each property. For example, a User object includes, but is not limited to, the following properties:

- Login Name (the user's login name, such as THERBON)

- Telephone Number (most likely an office phone number)

- E-mail Address (such as THERBON @ WIDGETCO)

- Password Restrictions (such as minimum length, time between changes, and so on)

- Group Membership (what groups the user is a member of)

- Address (could be an office address and mail stop)

Figure 2-1 shows the relationship between objects, properties, and values.

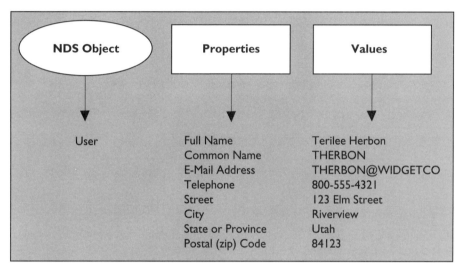

Figure 2-1. An NDS object consists of numerous properties with corresponding values.

In most cases, more than one value can be entered for a specific property. An example is the Telephone Number property for the NDS User object. In this property's fields you can enter values for a user's office phone number, home phone number, cellular phone number, and even a pager number. Once entered in the database, all of this vital information is available to users via the NetWare Directory.

Again, only those users or objects that have rights to this information will be able to access it. Rights can be assigned to objects and properties separately, if necessary. This flexibility in assigning rights makes NetWare's Directory very powerful.

After values are entered for the NDS object properties, you can perform a search for objects with specific values (similar to a query in a standard

21

database). For example, if you request information about all users whose phone numbers are in a specific area code, the Directory database could return all telephone numbers that contained the specified area code in their properties.

Another way of finding object information is by simply requesting information on a specific object. Of course, this method requires that you know some specific information about the object (such as its name or location). If this is the case, you can receive information on all properties of that object to which you have proper access rights.

Objects in the Directory Tree

The structure of the NDS database is implemented in a logical organization called a Directory tree. As described previously, this tree grows upside down with the roots at the top of the tree and the rest of the tree branching downward, as shown in Figure 2-2.

As you might expect, rights assigned to objects and properties in the Directory flow down through the tree. The importance of this concept becomes clearer as we discuss NDS objects in more detail.

The NDS Directory tree is made up of three types of objects:

- The [Root] object

- Container objects

- Leaf objects

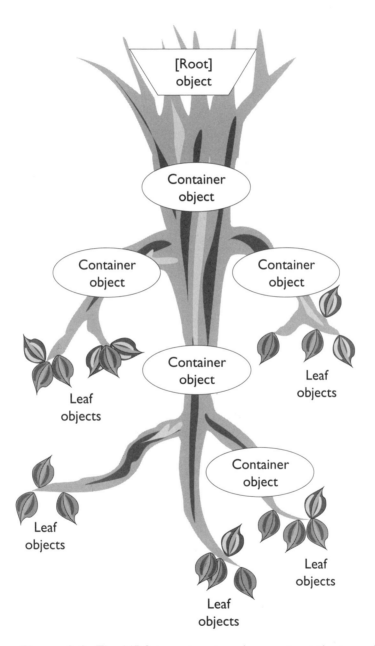

Figure 2-2. The NDS tree structure has roots at the top; all other objects branch downward from there.

The [Root] object

Since you cannot have a Directory tree without the [Root] object, the NetWare 4 installation program automatically creates [Root] and places it at the top of the Directory tree. The [Root] object cannot be renamed or deleted.

NOTE Do not confuse the [Root] object in a NetWare Directory tree with the root directory in the file system. In the file system, the root directory is equivalent to the volume level of the directory hierarchy. It bears no relation to the [Root] object in the Directory tree.

The [Root] object is not of much concern when you design the tree. It is created automatically, and it doesn't count as a "level" when you are planning how deep your tree should be. Yet it is an NDS object and, as such, [Root] can both have trustees and be assigned as a trustee. There are very few cases where this is necessary, and you should fully understand the implications before assigning rights to [Root] or making [Root] a trustee of another object. These implications are discussed in Chapter 3.

Container objects

Another important type of object in the Directory tree structure is the container object. Container objects hold (or contain) other NDS objects—both leaf objects and other container objects. However, container objects cannot hold the [Root] object.

Container objects provide a means of logically organizing all other objects in the Directory tree. Just as file system directories are used to group related files together, NDS container objects are used to group related items in the Directory tree.

In most cases, you will use only two kinds of container objects: Organization and Organizational Unit. The NDS Directory also supports

Country and Locality as container objects (as defined in the CCITT X.500 specification). However, in most situations these objects only add unnecessary complexity to the Directory tree. NDS is flexible enough that there should be no need to use either of these container objects. For these reasons, Country and Locality are not covered in this book.

Organization (O)

An Organization (O) container object organizes other objects in the Directory tree. For example, an Organization object can designate a corporation, a division within a company, a university or college with various departments, or a department with several project teams.

The Organization object also provides a convenient grouping that allows you to set defaults for all of the User objects you create in the Organization container.

NDS requires one or more Organization objects in every Directory tree. The installation program forces you to create at least one Organization object. Organization objects must be placed one level below the [Root] object.

Organizational Unit (OU)

The Organizational Unit (OU) object helps to organize leaf objects in the Directory tree. Organizational Unit objects can be used to designate a business unit within a company, a department within a division or university, or a project team within a department.

Like Organization objects, Organizational Units provide a convenient grouping so you can set defaults in a container-wide login script. You can also create a user template for User objects you want to create within the Organizational Unit container.

The use of Organizational Unit objects is optional in a Directory tree. When used in a Directory tree, Organizational Units must always be placed one level below an Organization or another Organizational Unit.

25

Leaf objects

NDS leaf objects are objects that do not contain any other objects. They represent actual network entities such as users, servers, printers, and computers. The following sections list and describe the different types of leaf objects available in NDS.

User-related leaf objects

A number of leaf objects deal with network users and groups.

User. A User object represents any specific person who logs in to and uses the network. A User object must be created for every user who needs to access the network.

When creating a User object, you can also create a file system "home" directory for that user and grant the user rights to this directory. NetWare 4 also allows you to define a User_Template object to provide new users with a set of default settings that you have chosen.

Group. The Group object represents a number of User objects together. This object assigns rights to a group of users as a whole, rather than just to individual users. The users listed as members of a group can be located anywhere in the Directory tree. The rights assigned to a Group object are granted to the individual users who belong to that group, no matter where they are located in the Directory tree.

You can also use groups to simplify the granting of rights to applications. For example, if you have installed WordPerfect on your network, each user who wants to access the program needs certain rights to the WordPerfect directories and files. By creating a Group object called WP Users, you can grant the appropriate rights to that object. Any User object can then be made a member of the WP Users group and automatically receive the necessary rights to run the application.

Profile. A Profile object contains a profile script, which is a type of login script. When listed as a property of a User object, the Profile object's script is executed whenever that user logs in to the network. It is executed after the system (container) login script, but before the user login script.

You can create a Profile object for any set of users (such as a group) who need to share common login script commands, but who are not necessarily located in the same Directory container. The Profile object can also be used for any users who are a subset of other users located in the same container.

Organizational Role. The Organizational Role object is used to define a position, or "role," within an organization. The person holding this position may change frequently, but the actual responsibilities of the position do not change. The Organizational Role object is also useful when two or more different people "share" the same job (for example, when there is a day shift and a night shift).

Any User object can be assigned to be an occupant of the Organizational Role object. Any occupant of an Organizational Role receives the same rights that were granted to the Organizational Role object.

For example, suppose you want someone to have the responsibility of being Print Manager for the Sales department, but you do not want the same person to have to handle the job for more than a one-month period. You could create an Organizational Role object called Print Manager and grant that object all object rights to the Printer, Print Queue, and Print Server objects in the Sales department's part of the Directory tree. You might also grant Print Manager property rights to the Print Job Configuration property of all users in that part of the Directory tree. This setup allows the Print Manager Organizational Role object to manage all printing in the Sales container, without having to grant these rights to individual users. It will be easy to change them later as job responsibilities are shifted.

Server-related leaf objects

The following leaf objects are related specifically to NetWare servers and volumes.

NetWare Server. A NetWare Server object represents a physical NetWare 4 server on your network. Whenever a NetWare 4 server is installed in the tree, a NetWare Server object is automatically created.

The NetWare Server object's properties are used to store information about the server. This information can include the server's location on the wire, the server's physical location, what services the server can provide, and so on.

In addition to storing NetWare server information, this object is also referred to by other objects in the Directory. For example, the NDS Volume object points to the NetWare Server object to find the location of a physical volume on the network. The Directory Map object points to the NetWare Server object to find the file system directory it needs to access. Server objects are used by Directory Services itself to track the location of all servers and replicas.

The NetWare Server object ties the physical server on the network to the Directory tree. Without the NetWare Server object, you cannot access file systems that reside on the server's volumes.

The NetWare Server object can also be used for strictly informational purposes. For example, you could create NetWare Server objects for servers not in the Directory tree (such as 3.11 servers not in the tree). These non-NetWare 4 servers would then show up in the Directory when you browse the tree.

Volume. Each NDS Volume object represents a physical volume on the network. The NetWare 4 INSTALL.NLM automatically creates a Volume object at installation time for every physical volume on a server.

The Volume object's properties store information about which NetWare server the physical volume is located on, as well as the name given when the volume was initialized (such as SYS or VOL1). When a Volume object is created during installation, the necessary information is placed in the Volume object's properties by default. The properties in the Volume object are also used for mapping network drives.

Directory Map. The NDS Directory Map object represents a specific file system directory path or file on a specified server. The Directory Map objects are used in login scripts to point to file system directories that contain frequently accessed applications or files. The NetWare MAP utility uses the Directory Map object for mapping drive paths.

As an example of using the Directory Map object, suppose you have a directory that contains a frequently used application, such as a spreadsheet. Before NetWare 4, you would probably map a search drive to that directory in all login scripts you create. If you later upgraded to a newer version of the spreadsheet and renamed the directory, you would typically have to change the mapping in every login script that contains the mapping to the application's directory.

By using the Directory Map object, you avoid the necessity of changing every user's login script individually. Instead, you just change the Directory Map object, and all of the search mappings in your users' login scripts are updated to find the new version automatically.

Printer-related leaf objects

Several NDS leaf objects are related to NetWare's print services. These objects are created and controlled using NetWare's print utilities (PCONSOLE and others).

Printer. The NDS Printer object represents a physical printing device on the network. A Printer object must be created for every printer on the network.

Print Queue. The NDS Print Queue object represents a network print queue. Every print queue on the network must have its own Print Queue object.

Print Server. The NDS Print Server object represents a network print server. As with print queues, every print server on the network must have its own Print Server object.

Informational leaf objects

The following leaf objects are used only for the purpose of storing network resource information. They have absolutely no effect on network operation.

AFP Server. The AFP Server object represents an AppleTalk Filing Protocol-based server on your network. Currently, the AFP Server leaf object provides no functionality. It is used only to store information about the server, such as network address, operators, and users.

If you have more than one AFP Server on your network, create a separate AFP Server leaf object to represent each one.

Computer. The NDS Computer object represents a nonserver computer, usually a workstation or router, that resides on the network. This object is used to store such information as the computer's network address, serial number, or the person responsible for the computer.

Miscellaneous leaf objects

This section lists the remaining types of NDS leaf objects.

Alias. An NDS Alias object refers (or points) to another NDS object in the Directory tree and makes it appear as if the object to which the Alias object points actually exists in the Directory tree at the point where the Alias object is created.

Aliases can be used in a variety of ways. For instance, if users in one Organizational Unit access a server in another OU often, it may be convenient to create an Alias object for that server in their OU. That way, the server can be referenced relative to a local context that is already set for those users. They don't have to "walk" the tree to find the server in the other OU.

Aliases can also simplify searches of the Directory. For example, you could create aliases in a single OU for all modems on the network. Then users only have to search one OU to obtain information about all available modems.

Bindery Object. An NDS Bindery Object represents a non-NDS object placed in the Directory tree by one of the NetWare various upgrade or migration utilities. The NDS Bindery Object is used only to provide backward compatibility with bindery-oriented utilities that create their own object type.

You cannot create a Bindery Object. Although you can see it in the Directory tree, a Bindery Object cannot be converted into an NDS object. However, NetWare 4 provides a set of APIs to allow developers to create their own object types if necessary.

Bindery Queue. The NDS Bindery Queue object represents a non-NDS queue (such as a bindery-based print queue) placed in the Directory tree by one of the NetWare upgrade or migration utilities. The Bindery Queue object is also used by NDS to provide backward compatibility with bindery-oriented utilities.

As with the Bindery Object, you cannot create a Bindery Queue object. It can be seen in the Directory tree, but it cannot be converted to an NDS object.

Unknown. An Unknown object represents any NDS object that has been invalidated and cannot be identified as belonging to any of the other identified object classes.

Possible NDS Tree Configurations

In a Directory tree, you can place container objects and leaf objects in just about any type of configuration that meets your needs. You are not limited to only one container object. In fact, most Directory trees have numerous container objects.

NDS requires only that you have at least one Organization object in the tree. Thus the simplest possible Directory tree would consist of a single Organization object with all leaf objects created within that container, as shown in Figure 2-3.

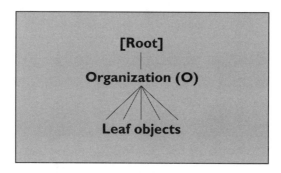

Figure 2-3. A simple Directory tree with one Organization object.

You can have only *one* level of Organization objects in a Directory tree. Underneath that level, you can add as many levels of Organizational Unit objects as you need. You can also create as many subordinate Organizational Units as you need under a single Organization. Figure 2-4 shows two variations on our simple Directory tree (Figure 2-3) that illustrate these concepts.

Although the number of OU levels you can have is theoretically unlimited, there are several practical issues to consider. First, the total length of the full "path" name from an OU up the tree to the O is limited to 512 bytes (256 Unicode characters). Second, the number of OU levels in the tree can affect how easily users can login from other locations on the network.

Third, adding too many levels can affect performance. For these reasons, you should carefully consider how many levels you really need and avoid adding unnecessary depth to the tree.

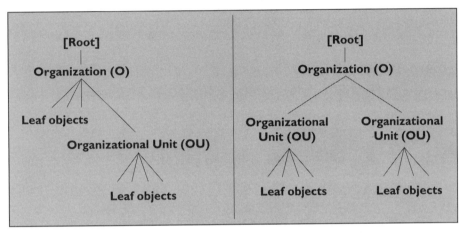

Figure 2-4. Other Organizational Units and leaf objects can be added as needed to form the Directory tree.

These simple examples give you a feel for the different ways in which objects can be laid out to form the Directory tree. Chapter 7 gives more specific guidelines on how to design the tree and place objects for varying network needs.

NDS Context and Object Names

One of the new terms associated with NetWare 4 and Directory Services is *context*. In NDS, your context refers to your current location in the Directory tree. For example, look at the sample Directory tree shown in Figure 2-5.

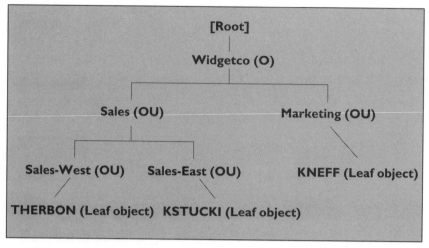

Figure 2-5: Example of various contexts in a Directory tree.

In this tree, the context for user THERBON would be:

```
Sales-West.Sales.Widgetco
```

The context for user KNEFF would be:

```
Marketing.Widgetco
```

The context is important for the Directory to locate specified network resources, such as servers and printers, within the tree. It is also important to a user logging in to the network.

Whenever a user logs in to the network, that user automatically requests authentication services. Based on the user's current context and the login name the user provides, authentication services must find a User object that matches that login name. NDS then uses the property values associated with the specified user object to validate the user's password and other user account restrictions. When this authentication process is successfully completed, the user is authenticated as a valid network user and has full access to all network resources he or she has proper access rights to use.

Context is also important when you are creating users. NetWare 4 users (those using NDS client software on their workstations rather than bindery emulation) can be created anywhere in the Directory tree. However, to login, NDS users must know their exact NDS context. To make this easier, you can specify users' contexts in their workstation NET.CFG file when you install the NetWare 4 client software. By setting the NDS context in the NET.CFG file, users automatically are placed in their correct context every time they login from their workstation. (This NET.CFG setting is described in Chapter 10.)

Users with non-NetWare 4 workstations (bindery clients) must be created in the container where the bindery emulation context is set for their primary server. By default, bindery emulation is enabled on all NetWare 4 servers during installation. Bindery emulation users do not need to know their context because they are logging into a server (as in previous version of NetWare), rather than logging into the Directory tree. (For more information on bindery emulation, see Chapter 6.)

Common name

Most leaf objects in the Directory tree have a *common name* (CN). A User object's common name is usually the same as the login name displayed in the Directory tree. For example, in Figure 2-6 the common name for Terilee Herbon's User object is THERBON.

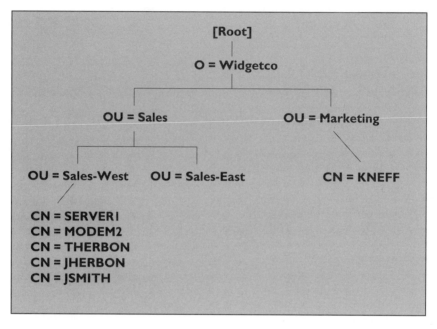

Figure 2-6: Example of a Directory tree showing common names.

Other leaf objects (such as Printer objects and Server objects) also have common names displayed in the Directory tree.

Complete name

The entire path from an object, up to but not including the [Root] of the Directory tree, forms the object's *complete name*. Thus, the complete name of leaf object THERBON in Organizational Unit Sales-West in Organizational Unit Sales in Organization Widgetco would be properly denoted as:

```
THERBON.Sales-West.Sales.Widgetco
```

The order of the objects in a complete name is critical. The common name comes first, followed by the OUs (in ascending order, as you walk up the tree), and ending with the Organization. It is not necessary to specify [Root] as part of an object's name.

To avoid Directory conflicts, the complete name of each object must be unique. Two leaf objects with the same common name can exist in different containers, but all object names in the same container must be distinct.

Distinguished, or typeful names

The complete name shown above for THERBON is an example of a "typeless" name, because the object types (CN, OU, and O) are not specifically included.

In some cases, it might be necessary to include the type of each of the objects when specifying a complete name. This is called a distinguished, or typeful name because it includes the specific classes of objects to which you are referring, such as a leaf object's common name, OU objects, and O objects.

The following example shows how to express a typeless name as a typeful or distinguished name. To use the previous example, you would express

```
THERBON.Sales-West.Sales.Widgetco
```

as

```
CN=THERBON.OU=Sales-West.OU=Sales.O=Widgetco
```

where CN is the common name of the leaf object, OU is the Organizational Unit name or names (two in this case), and O is the Organization name.

Most likely, you will need to use typeful names only rarely, if at all. If you are referring to an object that is in the same container object as your User object, you can refer to the specified object by its common name, rather than by its complete name. In Figure 2-6, if User object THERBON, located in Sales-West.Sales.Widgetco wants information about User object JSMITH, located in the same context, THERBON could simply refer to the User object as JSMITH.

Whenever you move from one container object to another, your Directory context is changed. When you change contexts, you must specify the complete name of the container object to which you are changing your context. You may have to include the types of the objects when specifying the new context. Thus, THERBON would refer to User object KNEFF in Marketing.Widgetco as

```
CN=KNEFF.OU=Marketing.O=Widgetco
```

Making object names unique

When designing your Directory tree, remember that all *complete* names of objects must be unique within a Directory tree. All container and object names must be unique within the container where they reside.

The Directory only recognizes unique names within a container. If you try to create two users with identical common names in the same container, you will run into problems. For example, suppose you have assigned user Jane Ann Doe the common name of JDOE in the Sales container. If you then assign user Jane Marie Doe the common name JDOE in the same container, the Directory would treat both users as one and the same, since the Directory only recognizes one JDOE in that container. This would prevent the two users from having unique rights and access to Directory resources.

In circumstances such as this, it is a good practice to include the user's middle initial (or similar unique feature) to create distinct user names. For Jane Ann Doe and Jane Marie Doe, you could create unique user objects named JADOE and JMDOE.

To ensure that User object names are unique, you might want to use e-mail naming conventions or actual e-mail names as users' common names.

The same unique naming rules also hold true for Directory containers, resources, and all other objects. To prevent conflicts, be sure each user, resource, and container that resides in the same container has a unique name.

If you set up multiple Directory trees (such as on a test network), each tree name should be unique to avoid problems.

Creating object-naming guidelines

While NetWare Directory Services does not require any special naming conventions, we recommend that you formulate some naming conventions that are simple to decipher, and use them consistently across your network. Remember, simplicity is a key to efficient planning when dealing with NDS.

In NetWare 4.0 and 4.01, you cannot easily change the name of a container object (O or OU) once it is named. To avoid possible problems, you should carefully plan the names of your container objects and their location in the Directory structure before implementing your Directory tree. Later releases of NetWare 4 will provide the ability to rename a container, but it is still best to plan your naming strategy in advance.

To keep the Directory tree easy to traverse and more efficient, names of containers should be short, meaningful, and easy to remember. Since the full distinguished name of an object is sent across the wire for any changes to that object, using short container names lessens the amount of data sent around during Directory synchronizations.

Use mixed case and spaces in object names to make them more readable. You are no longer limited to uppercase, single-word names such as NYMKTG. When entering names at the command line, substitute underscores for spaces, such as NY_Mktg. (In NDS, underscores equate to spaces.)

Try to come up with a simple set of naming conventions for User objects, such as using e-mail names or login names. As suggested above, you might name all of the User objects by taking the initial of the user's first and middle names, followed by the user's last name. Another option might be to use the User object's last name, followed by the first and middle initials.

Be consistent in naming network devices as well. For example, you could name your printers with specified prefixes, followed by such information as the specified printer's physical location. For example, if you have an Apple LaserWriter printer located in Corporate Publications, and you have an HPII located in the same department, you might name the Apple LaserWriter APL followed by an underscore (_) followed by a descriptor. The HPII would be named in the same fashion. Thus the Apple LaserWriter printer would be named APL_CorpPubs and the HPII would be named HPII_CorpPubs. These names easily identify both the type and physical location of the printers.

For general naming of Directory objects, we recommend you select a method that is simple to remember and that will help your users easily identify resources (different types of printers, modems, workstations, and so on). This will make Directory searches easier for average users who do not necessarily know all of the specifics of a resource they need to use.

For example, suppose a writer needs to access a printer near his desk, but doesn't know the specifics of the printer (such as the fact that the printer contains a cartridge with 63 different fonts). As long as the writer knows that the printer is an Apple LaserWriter, he can do a search for all Apple LaserWriters he has rights to. From the resulting list, he can determine which printer he wants to use. This works best if you use simple naming conventions as suggested.

Keep your naming conventions consistent across the network so they are easy for everyone to decipher and use. Below is a list of possible prefixes for common network resources:

APL_	Apple LaserWriter printer
HPL_	Hewlett Packard LaserJet printer
CPMQ_	Compaq PageMarq printer
PLOT_	Plotter
NPQ_	NetWare print queue
NPS_	NetWare print server
HM_	Hayes modem
HCM_	Hayes-compatible modem
CPQ_	Compaq workstation
PS2_	IBM PS/2 workstation

The prefixes above are only the first part of the name. You must still put a specific name, location, or identifier after the underscore (_) in the prefix. For example, you might use

```
APL_Gamal's Desk
```

to denote the Apple LaserWriter printer that is physically located near Gamal's desk.

These are just a few examples of how you might want to name your network resources to make resource searches and access easier for your users. Feel free to come up with your own naming conventions that make sense for your network.

Whatever you decide, be sure to document all of the naming conventions you will use on your network and provide a copy of these standards to all administrators of your network (or sections of your network). Appendix A contains an example of an NDS Naming Standards Document you can adapt for your needs.

Summary

In this chapter, we have learned more about the structure of the NDS Directory tree. We have discussed the three main categories of objects: [Root], container, and leaf objects. Every Directory tree must have a [Root] object, which is created automatically by the NetWare 4 installation program and cannot be renamed or deleted. Container objects hold other objects, and there are two main types: Organization (O) and Organizational Unit (OU). Every tree must have at least one Organization object, whereas OUs are optional. Leaf objects represent actual resources, devices, or users on the network. They are assigned a common name (CN).

Your NDS context is where you currently are within the Directory tree. The full path as you traverse the tree from an object up to the [Root] forms the object's complete name. An object can be represented either as a typeless name (such as THERBON.Sales-West.Sales.Widgetco) or as a typeful name that includes object type designations (such as CN=THERBON.OU=Sales-West.OU=Sales.O=Widgetco).

To avoid conflicts, the complete name of each object in the Directory tree must be unique. It is recommended that you establish naming conventions for all objects in the tree. Standardized naming conventions allow you to more fully exploit the power of NDS. When naming conventions are used in a consistent manner, browsing and searching in the Directory is quicker and easier for both users and network administrators.

NDS Access Control and Security Features

O ne of the strongest features in NetWare has always been the security it provides, both for the file system and for other network resources. In NetWare 4, overall security has been enhanced with the addition of features such as authentication, auditing, and NDS access control.

This chapter provides an overview of these features and explains how NetWare 4 sets up most of the NDS access control by default. This information should give you enough background on security considerations for designing your Directory tree. Chapter 11 covers more advanced access control concepts and explains how to assign NDS rights for specialized needs.

NetWare 4 Security

NetWare 4 retains the powerful file system security features used in previous versions of NetWare. With the introduction of NetWare Directory Services, a new level of security is necessary to control access to NDS objects and their properties. Thus there are four distinct sets, or levels, of access rights in NetWare 4:

- File system directory rights
- File system file rights
- NDS object rights
- NDS property rights

File system rights will be familiar to users of NetWare 2 and 3. These are the trustee rights (Read, Write, Create, Erase, and so on) that control what you can do to files and directories in the NetWare file system. This type of security enables users to run applications and access data files. Within the bindery, previous versions of NetWare had very limited access levels to bindery objects.

NetWare 4 adds NDS object rights and NDS property rights, which govern access to the objects within the Directory tree. This type of security enables administrators to maintain the NDS database and its objects. The tasks these rights allow include creating users, editing login scripts, assigning trustee rights, designating workgroup managers or console operators, and creating printers and print servers.

For the most part, file system security and NDS security do not affect each other. This independence allows file-system administration to be totally separate from NDS administration, if your network needs warrant such a division of responsibility.

Since this book is about NetWare Directory Services, I'll focus mainly on the new NDS rights. Refer to the NetWare documentation for more information about file system rights.

Authentication

In NetWare 4, *authentication* is the foundation for network-wide security. The authentication process allows objects to prove their identities prior to receiving access to information or services. Without a method for identifying users and applications, there is no way to enforce other security systems such as access control.

Authentication occurs in two different ways on the network:

1. **Initial authentication** occurs when a user first logs into the network. At this time, the user supplies a login name and a password. The authentication and verification operations are performed behind the scenes.

2. **Background authentication** refers to subsequent authentication to additional services after the initial login. The user does not need to retype a password. Background authentication is also transparent to users.

Authentication is session oriented. A client's digital signature—the data that provides the basis of the authentication—is valid only for the duration of the current login session. If the authentication data is somehow captured, only the current sessions can be compromised. The data cannot be applied to later sessions. The critical data that creates authenticated messages for a particular user is never transmitted across the wire.

Authentication is a network service. Other applications can use the authentication services APIs to set up authenticated sessions between their own services and clients.

Finally, we should note that NetWare's authentication is based on RSA cryptography. This is an asymmetrical encryption scheme that involves a public key and a private key. Data is encrypted with one key and decrypted with the other. The relationship between these keys is mathematically complex and it is very difficult to determine the value of one key from the other. RSA encryption technology has been in use for over 10 years, and no one has yet been able to defeat it.

Auditing

Auditing is a process in which a designated user examines an organization's records to ensure that confidential data is secure and that transactions are handled correctly. Organizations normally call on independent auditors so the procedure will be unbiased and accurate.

In NetWare 4, the overall auditing capabilities have been greatly enhanced. An AUDITCON utility is provided to audit server events (involving users and the file system), and Directory Services events. Records concerning server and user events are stored in an audit log file in the SYS volume of the server being audited. Only an authorized auditor has access to the audit file. This auditor is a separate entity from the network administrator.

Refer to the NetWare 4 documentation for more information about auditing features.

Access Control for the Directory Tree

Access to the objects within the Directory tree is governed by NDS object rights and NDS property rights. In this book, we'll refer to these rights as object and property rights.

In NDS, object and property rights are assigned separately to provide enhanced security and better access control over the information (properties) associated with NDS objects. Following is a brief overview of object and property rights.

NOTE Keep in mind that object and property rights apply only to the NetWare Directory tree, not to the file system directories or files.

Object rights

Object rights control what a trustee is allowed to do to the object. The object rights are listed in Figure 3-1.

Browse	Allows a trustee to see the object in the Directory tree.
Create	Allows a trustee to create a new object below the specified object in the Directory tree. Create applies only to container objects.
Delete	Allows a trustee to delete the object from the Directory tree. Only leaf objects and empty container objects can be deleted.
Rename	Allows a trustee to change the name of the object Rename applies only to leaf objects.
Supervisor	Grants all object access privileges and all rights to the object's properties.

Figure 3-1. NDS object rights

These rights control access to an NDS object as a single piece of the Directory tree, but they do not allow access to the specific information stored within that object (the object's properties). The one exception is the Supervisor object right, which applies to both the object itself and to the object's properties.

In general, object rights are primarily of use only to the NDS administrator for creating, deleting, and renaming objects in the tree. Most users need only the Browse object right so they can see objects in the tree. They can then perform Directory searches and walk the tree to find a particular context. When created, a User object is automatically given the Browse right to itself so that the user can see his or her own object in the tree.

Property Rights

Property rights control a trustee's access to specific information associated with the object (in the object's properties). NDS property rights are listed in Figure 3-2.

Property rights apply only to NDS object properties and their values, not to the objects themselves. Many properties can have multiple values, and rights for a given property apply to all of its values. Both users and NDS administrators can be granted property rights to control their ability to see and manipulate the values of an object's property.

Objects have as many properties as specified in the NetWare Directory Services schema. The User object, for example, has over 50 properties ranging from Account Balance to UID. (Appendix A of the NetWare 4.0 *Utilities Reference* manual contains tables of all NDS objects and their associated properties.)

Compare	Allows a trustee to compare a value to the value of the property, but does not allow the trustee to see the value.
Read	Allows a trustee to read the values of the property. Read also allows compare operations even if the Compare right is not explicitly granted.
Write	Allows a trustee to add, change, or remove any values of the property.
Add/Delete Self	Allows the trustee to add or remove itself as a value of the property, without affecting any other values. This is useful for properties such as group lists or mail delivery lists.
Supervisor	Grants all rights to the property.

Figure 3-2. NDS property rights

Property rights can be assigned to all properties of an object, or to selected properties only. For example, one of the User object's properties is Telephone Number. If you use this property to store the user's telephone number, you can prevent another person from seeing the specified telephone number by not granting that person the Read right to that property. However, at the same time you can allow that person to view other properties, such as the user's e-mail address. This ability to control access to properties affords you a great deal of flexibility in deciding what Directory information others can see.

Access Control Lists

One property of all NDS objects is the Access Control List (ACL). The ACL is a special property that stores information about who can access the object and its properties. An object's ACL lists three types of information:

1. Who has rights to the object (the trustees)

2. What rights the trustees have (the rights assignments)

3. The object's Inherited Rights Filter (explanation follows)

It is important to understand that an object's ACL defines which *other* objects in the Directory can access that object and its properties. It does not list what that object might have rights to.

As an example of how the ACL works, consider a Printer object. Any object listed in the Printer object's ACL is a trustee of that Printer object and thus has at least some rights to that specific printer. To grant a user rights to the Printer object, go to the Printer object and make the user a trustee with the desired rights. You would not go to the User object and make the printer a trustee of that user.

Each object listed in a specified object's ACL can have different rights to that object's properties. For example, if 20 users are listed in a modem object's ACL as trustees, each of those users could conceivably be assigned different rights to that modem object and its various properties. However, in a working network environment, chances are high that at least some of the users will have the same or similar rights to the specified modem and its various properties.

Each ACL value can specify rights in one of the following ways:

- For the object itself (referred to simply as object rights)

- For all properties of that object (referred to in this book as All Properties after the option in the NWAdmin utility)

- For a specific property or properties of the object (NWAdmin also has a Selected Properties option)

Since the ACL is itself a property of an object, the ACL can have a trustee assignment to itself as one of its values. If the trustee has the Write right to the ACL, that trustee can modify any of the rights of the object.

To change a trustee's access to an object, you have to change the trustee's entry in that object's ACL. Only trustees with the Write (or Supervisor) property right for the ACL property can change a trustee's rights assignments or the Inherited Rights Filter.

Inherited rights

As is typical in a hierarchical tree structure, NDS object and property rights assigned in the upper levels of the Directory tree flow down through the branches below. When rights flow down like this, they are known as inherited rights.

The concept of inheritance should be familiar to those who understand how rights flow in NetWare's file system directory structure. With proper planning, you can take advantage of inheritance to minimize the number of explicit NDS trustee assignments you need to make.

The only NDS rights that can be inherited are object rights and property rights you assign to the All Properties option. Property rights assigned to a single property or selected properties do *not* flow down the tree to other objects. This is because a specific property usually only applies to a certain type of object. For example, the Telephone property of a User object makes no sense for a Printer or Organizational Unit object.

When an object has more than one specific trustee assignment to other objects at different levels of the tree, only the lowest-level assignment is considered in determining inheritance. NDS ignores any rights assignment above that. For example, if we grant User A the Browse object rights to container OU=Sales and only Rename and Delete rights to container

OU=Sales-West (under Sales), User A has Rename and Delete rights to all objects below OU=Sales-West. As you design your tree, you can control inheritance for a specific user by making multiple assignments.

Inherited Rights Filter

Sometimes you need to prevent the inheritance of specific rights to a branch of the tree or to a certain leaf object. The Inherited Rights Filter (IRF) can block any or all NDS rights so that objects cannot inherit them from parent objects, as shown in Figure 3-3.

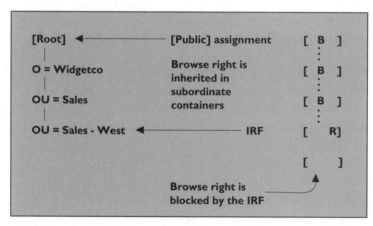

Figure 3-3. The Inherited Rights Filter blocks the flow of NDS rights to lower levels of the tree.

Inherited Rights Filters are similar in function to the rights-filtering capability in the NetWare file system. IRFs are available to every Object rights and All Properties rights assignments, as well as for specific property rights assignments.

Unlike trustee assignments, IRFs do not grant rights. The IRF exists for the sole purpose of revoking or blocking rights. For every object that has no explicit trustee assignment, the IRF allows only the specified rights to take effect (if they are inherited from parent objects). On the other hand, specific trustee assignments for both object and property rights override any IRF restrictions *for like rights*.

An easy way to keep this all straight is to remember that IRFs only affect rights being inherited *from above*. They do not affect any rights granted at the level where you set up the IRF.

The one exception in IRFs is that a property IRF cannot block an inherited Supervisor *object* right. If you grant the Supervisor object rights to an object, all property rights are automatically granted as well.

Security equivalences

In NetWare 4, the security equivalence feature has been significantly enhanced. Security equivalence is a quick and easy way to give the rights assigned to one object to any other object on the network. This is useful when, for example, a user in one part of an organization (User A) needs access to another user's files (User B). All you have to do is add User A to User B's Security Equivalence List, which is one of the User object's properties. To add a security equivalence, you need the Write rights to the ACL of the object.

Some security equivalences exist as system defaults and cannot be changed or revoked. All objects in the Directory tree are security equivalent to:

- The [Root] object

- Each container object in the direct path from [Root] down to the object's container

- The [Public] trustee

The equivalence to [Root], and to every container (O and OU) from there down to the container an object is in, makes it possible to use container objects as "groups" when assigning access rights. I'll explain more about this in a later section of this chapter.

The [Public] trustee is not an object, but rather a special trustee that can be added to any object (as well as to file system directories and files). It is used by objects that have not yet authenticated to NDS to find out information about the Directory and network resources without using up a licensed connection slot. Thus [Public] is the counterpart of "attached but not logged in" in bindery-based NetWare.

When NetWare 4 is first installed, the [Public] trustee is granted the Browse right at the [Root] level of the Directory tree. Since all other objects are security equivalent to the [Public] trustee, they can "walk" or browse the tree. This is what allows users to change contexts with the CX command even before they have logged in. Users need this ability to find their correct context. I'll discuss more about [Public] later in this chapter.

Granting rights to container objects

An interesting and useful facet of NDS security is that you can grant rights to container objects. When defining security in the Directory tree, you can think of a container object as a "natural group." All objects and subcontainers in a container are automatically part of the group without having to be explicitly added to a membership list. Thus objects in a container receive an implied security equivalence to that container, gaining all trustee rights of the container as if they were their own.

Rights assigned to a container flow down to subcontainers. This is often called *ancestral inheritance,* but it is separate from what we normally think of as inheritance. You cannot prevent a user in a container from receiving the rights assigned to that container (either with an IRF or by any other means). You can place an IRF on any object in a container below that, and the rules of inheritance apply.

Generally, you grant rights to an OU container to assign file system rights. For example, you could give OU=Pubs an explicit trustee assignment to SYS:APPS\WP. All users in that OU and below would also receive the same trustee rights. This is similar to creating a group called PUBS, making everyone a member, and assigning the file system rights to the group.

There are cases when NDS rights can be assigned to a container as well. For example, if you assign a container the Read property right to its Login Script property, all users in that container can run the container login script.

Effective rights

As you can see, there are several ways to define rights in the Directory tree. The combination of rights granted from inheritance, trustee assignments in the ACL, and security equivalences determine an object's *effective rights*. Effective rights are what ultimately control an object's access to another object and its properties.

Effective rights calculation in NetWare 4 is basically the same as in previous versions of NetWare. However, with NDS you now have several other sources to consider besides the traditional inherited rights, group assignments, explicit trustee assignments, and security equivalences. These include equivalence to the [Public] trustee and [Root] object, rights assigned to containers, and Organizational Roles. Chapter 11 will discuss rights calculation in more detail.

Administering NDS Access Control

This quick overview of NDS security, with its seemingly endless possibilities and combinations of rights, may have you dreading the prospect of having to administer access control in your Directory tree. Don't panic. Under normal circumstances, it is not necessary to manually set up an elaborate NDS security structure. NetWare 4 does most of the work for you with its defaults. These defaults should be adequate for users to fully exploit the advantages of Directory Services.

The following sections explain what you need to understand about NDS administration when designing the Directory tree. I'll talk about User object Admin and how to delegate administrative responsibility at various levels of the tree. I'll also review the NDS access control defaults and introduce a few situations where you might need to implement additional rights assignments.

User object Admin

The NDS User object known as Admin is an important object in the NetWare 4 environment. Admin can initially be thought of as the network supervisor. (The term *network supervisor* is used here to refer to the person responsible for setting up the NetWare 4 network.)

NetWare creates a single Admin object (by default) during the installation of the first NetWare 4 server. This is the User object the network supervisor will use the first time he or she logs in to the NetWare 4 network.

 The User object Admin does not have any special significance like that associated with SUPERVISOR in previous versions of NetWare. Admin is granted rights to create and manage all objects simply because it is the first object created.

When Admin is created on the first NetWare 4 server installed, it receives a trustee assignment of Supervisor rights to the [Root] object of the Directory tree. As a result, Admin has all rights to every object and property in the Directory tree. Admin initially needs complete control over the Directory tree so it can be used to set up the rest of the tree.

As part of the default rights assignment, Admin also receives the Supervisor object right to each NetWare Server object created in the tree. This gives Admin the Supervisor right to the file system root directory of all volumes attached to the server. Thus Admin can manage all of the file system directories and files on every volume in the Directory tree.

Delegating administrative responsibility

Just because NetWare 4 creates only one Admin object does not mean you are limited to having only one network supervisor. As you design and implement your Directory tree, you will likely have several network supervisors, each administering a different part of the Directory tree.

In large, global Directory trees, there may be containers that represent geographically separate entities. In these cases, it is usually more convenient to have local Directory administrators than only one central administrator. You wouldn't want an administrator in Cody, Wyoming to manage an entire global network over wide area links. At the same time, the administrator in Wyoming probably knows the local environment and users better than someone in Europe would.

As User objects are created in the Directory, Admin can grant the Supervisor object right to selected objects or even to entire subtrees in the Directory. Objects that receive the Supervisor object right can then create and manage other container objects and their leaf objects. Thus Directory control and management can be as centralized or as dispersed as your needs dictate.

If you assign another User object the Supervisor object right to the [Root] object, you can rename or even delete the User object Admin. Heed the following warning before doing this!

WARNING

Never delete User object Admin without having previously assigned the Supervisor right to the [Root] object. The results can be disastrous, as you will have no supervisory control of the Directory tree.

This warning also applies to other sections of the Directory tree (besides the [Root]) where you might have a User object Admin defined. Wherever you define an Admin object, be sure you also have a User object with explicit Admin rights (not equivalences) at that level in the tree.

If you inadvertently lose control over all or part of your tree by deleting Admin, contact Novell Technical Support at 1-800-NET-WARE (or 1-801-429-5588) for a workaround procedure.

Default NDS rights assignments

To provide basic network functionality, the following rights are granted by default:

- On the first NetWare 4 server installed, Admin is created and receives a trustee assignment of the Supervisor object right to the [Root] of the Directory tree. This allows Admin to initially administer the rest of the tree.

  Admin also receives the Supervisor object right to each NetWare Server object created in the tree. This gives Admin the Supervisor right to the file system root directory of all volumes attached to the server.

- On each server, the SYS Volume object's container object is granted Read and File Scan rights to the volume's SYS:PUBLIC directory. This allows all users created in the same container object to access all utilities located in the SYS:PUBLIC directory.

- [Public] has the Browse object right to [Root]. Since all objects are security equivalent to [Public], this allows anyone to browse the entire Directory tree before they login.

- When a user is created as a leaf object in the Directory tree, the User object is given the Browse object right to itself so the user can see its own object in the tree. A User object is also granted the Read property right to All Properties, and Read and Write rights to its Login Script and Print Job Configuration properties. These allow users to view information about themselves, and modify their own login script and print job configurations.

There are other defaults that NetWare 4 sets up depending on which installation options you select. For example, if you choose to install the ElectroText documentation, the SYS volume's container is granted Read and File Scan rights to the SYS:DOC directory. Users in that container can then access the on-line manuals.

Additional access control considerations

You will notice that most of the defaults assume a container-level model of access control. In other words, it is assumed that users will be created in the same container as their most frequently accessed server. The default rights assignments allow users to login and use other system resources (such as print queues) defined in the same container. This is a good model to follow when designing your Directory tree.

Following are some final concepts you should consider when designing security for your Directory tree.

Use of the [Root] object

Because [Root] is an NDS object, it can have trustees and it can also be a trustee. However, you should give careful consideration before assigning trustee rights to the [Root] object or making [Root] a trustee of another object.

If you grant a trustee assignment to [Root], *every* object in the tree will have those same rights because trustee rights flow down the tree until filtered out by an IRF. In effect, you will have made *all* users security equivalent to [Root]. We have already seen some examples of this concept. One is the User object Admin, which by default receives a trustee assignment of Supervisor rights to the [Root] object. This gives Admin all rights to all objects and properties in the tree.

In a small network where all users need access to all servers, it may be appropriate to assign file system rights to SYS:PUBLIC and common application directories at the [Root] object level. It also lets users run the applications from a different server in case their primary server goes down.

On larger networks you should avoid assigning extensive NDS rights at the [Root] precisely because they flow down to all users. Most NDS rights are management rights that nonadministrative users don't need.

The [Root] object can also be a trustee of another object. Again, you should carefully consider the implications before making the [Root] object a trustee. If you make the [Root] object a trustee of another object, every object in the Directory tree will have the same trustee rights as the [Root] object. Again, you will have effectively made *all* users security equivalent to [Root].

More about the [Public] trustee

As explained earlier, [Public] is a special trustee used by anyone who is requesting authentication to the network, even prior to logging in.

Use caution when making [Public] trustee assignments, as the [Public] trustee's rights are given to all network users as soon as they are attached to the network. It is not necessary to login to receive these rights. By default, [Public] has the Browse object right to [Root]. This lets everyone move around in the tree to find the correct context for logging in.

While [Public] may seem reminiscent of the user GUEST and group EVERYONE in previous versions of NetWare, it is not exactly the same. There are better ways to implement tree-wide rights than by using the [Public] trustee. These methods are discussed in Chapter 11.

Summary

When used carefully, NDS access control can give you a great amount of control over your Directory and its objects. This chapter has given you a basic understanding of how NDS access control works and what the defaults are. This information should help you in designing your Directory tree.

Chapter 11 discusses how to assign NDS security to tailor the default rights assignments for specific needs. Informed use of access control lets you leverage the strengths of NDS and provides the control required for your particular environment and circumstances.

Partitions and Replicas

One of the most crucial parts of designing a Directory tree is deciding how to partition the database and where to replicate the partitions across the network. This chapter expands on the basic concepts presented earlier, describes the default partitioning and replication scheme imposed by NetWare 4, and discusses some cases in which you might need to deviate from the defaults.

The information in this chapter is intended to help you in designing your initial Directory tree. Partition management tasks, such as splitting and joining partitions and adding replicas, are discussed in Chapter 13.

NDS Partitions

In NetWare Directory Services, a *partition* is a logical division, or portion, of the global Directory database. Typically, the NDS database is made of several partitions, each of which is a distinct collection of container and leaf objects. It may be helpful to think of a partition as a subtree within the larger Directory tree. Partitions cannot overlap—a given object can exist in only one partition in the tree.

 NDS partitions are completely unrelated to the logical *disk* partitions created on NetWare hard disks during server installation. Do not confuse these two types of partitions.

N O T E

In NDS, partitions store and replicate Directory information. Each Directory partition consists of at least one container object, all objects contained within that object (including possibly other containers), and all data about those objects. They do not include any file system information. The partitioning of the Directory is completely transparent to users.

NDS Replicas

One of the biggest advantages of NDS is that it is a globally distributed database. This means that NDS is distributed across the network. To take full advantage of NDS and to provide fault tolerance for the Directory information, portions of the database should reside on many servers.

Rather than keep a copy of the entire database on every server (as was the case with the bindery), copies of each partition can be stored on many servers throughout the network. This distribution, or *replication,* of the NDS database virtually eliminates the risk of any single point of failure for the Directory and allows users to still login to the network if a server is down.

An NDS replica is simply a copy of an NDS partition. NetWare 4 allows you to create an unlimited number of replicas for each partition and store them on whatever network servers you choose.

Types of replicas

There are three types of NDS replicas:

1. Master replica

2. Read/Write replica

3. Read Only replica

Master replica

The Master replica is the first replica created for each NDS partition. Although you can have many other replicas of a partition, there can be only *one* Master replica of each partition in the Directory tree. The Master replica is also the only replica that can be used to change the structure of the Directory in relation to that specific partition. You can create a new partition in a Directory database only from the Master replica.

Read/Write replica

A Read/Write replica can be read for informational purposes, and it can be written to when it is necessary to change Directory information in that specific partition. For example, you can change a User object's information in a Read/Write replica and that change is perpetuated to all the other replicas of that partition, including the Master replica.

You can have more than one Read/Write replica of the same partition, but you cannot create new replicas of the partition from a Read/Write replica.

Read Only replica

The Read Only replica is just that: a replica from which you can only read Directory partition information. It cannot be written to, but it is updated to match information that has been changed on the Master or Read/Write replicas.

Purpose of replicas

In NetWare Directory Services, replicas serve two purposes:

1. Replicas provide Directory fault tolerance and thus minimize the risk of any single point of failure on the network.

2. Replicas provide faster Directory information access for networks running across WAN links.

You provide fault tolerance for the Directory by distributing NDS replicas across the network. If a disk crashes or a server goes down, a replica on another server elsewhere on the network can still authenticate users to the network and provide information on objects in the disabled server's partition. When the same Directory information (replica) is distributed on several servers, users are not dependent on any single server being up in order to authenticate them to the network or to provide available services.

NOTE

Directory replication (or Directory fault tolerance) does *not* provide fault tolerance for the file system. Only information about Directory objects is replicated. To provide file system fault tolerance, you must follow a process where you mirror or duplex your hard disks and enable the NetWare Transaction Tracking System (TTS). TTS must be enabled for NDS to work. For more information on file system fault tolerance, refer to your NetWare 4 product documentation.

Replication is also useful in environments where users communicate over WAN links to access network data or resources. Distributing replicas among servers on the network allows quick and reliable access, as Directory information is retrieved from the nearest available server that contains the specified information. Placing a replica of needed information on a server your users can access locally can decrease both access time and WAN traffic considerably.

I discuss the distribution of partitions in more detail later in this chapter, after looking at the NetWare 4 installation defaults.

Default Partitions and Replicas

It takes some planning to decide where to place your network partitions for most efficient use. Fortunately, the NetWare 4 installation program creates default Directory partitions for you. These defaults are designed to work well for the majority of Directory tree configurations.

NetWare 4 allows you the choice of using the default Directory partitions and replicas created by the installation program (defaults), or of using the Partition Manager Tool (GUI utility) or the PARTMGR (text utility) to change the partitions and replicas *after* your Directory tree is created.

Use the installation program's defaults until you understand the impact of partitioning, replication, and bindery emulation. Remember, NetWare 4 allows you the flexibility to change these options later.

T I P

The Root partition

The [Root] object, located at the top of the tree, is always included in the first NDS partition. The first NDS partition is created with the initial container object when you install the first NetWare 4 server. Thus, the first partition is known as the *root partition*.

Figure 4-1 shows an example of the default partition created for the first NetWare 4 server installed.

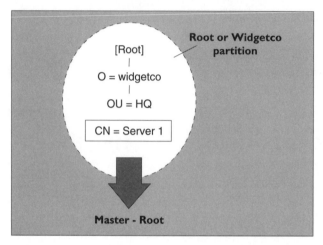

Figure 4-1. The root partition contains the [Root] object and is created when you install the first NetWare 4 server.

Directory partitions are identified by the name of the container closest to the root. So in Figure 4-1, the root partition is referred to as the Widgetco partition, because it contains the Organization named Widgetco.

If your Directory tree has just one Organization object without any Organizational Units, the Organization is automatically designated as the default partition. Since there are no other servers in the tree, the root partition is not yet replicated on any other server.

Subsequent partitions

As other Organizational Unit objects are created and NetWare 4 servers are installed in these containers, new partitions are created. NetWare 4 designates each new container object where a Server object is installed as a default Directory partition.

NetWare 4 places a Master replica of the Directory partition on the first server installed in a container object. All subsequent servers installed in the *same* container object receive a Read/Write replica of the Directory partition.

When you install a server in a new context, the NetWare 4 installation program creates a new partition, stores a Master replica on the new server, and puts a Read/Write replica on the new partition's parent partition, as shown in Figure 4-2.

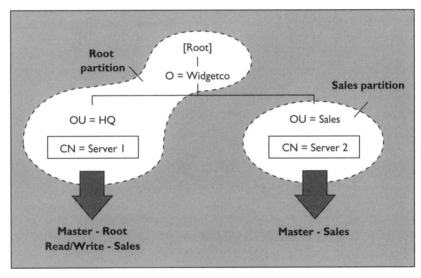

Figure 4-2. Default partitions with two servers.

The server's *bindery context* is also set automatically by the NetWare 4 installation program to the container object level where the server is installed. Bindery emulation needs a Read/Write replica on the server to work properly.

As you add servers to the tree, you will either install each one into an existing context, or you will create a new context. If you add a server to an existing context, the installation program asks if you want a Read/Write replica of that partition stored on the server. Doing so ensures that there are at least two replicas of that partition.

If you create a new context, the installation program creates a new partition, stores a Master replica of the new partition on the new server, and stores a Read/Write replica on the server containing the new server's parent context.

An example of default Directory partitions as might occur in a small Directory tree is shown in Figure 4-3. Note the difference between Directory partitions where a server object has been installed in a new context, versus a second server in an existing context.

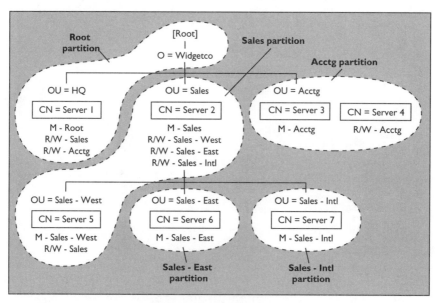

Figure 4-3. Sample Directory tree showing default partitions and replicas.

Possible limitations of the defaults

The default partition management scheme is adequate for simple Directory trees, and for many larger organizations—particularly those located at a single site with no WAN links.

There are two possible limitations to be aware of:

1. The defaults don't guarantee that the root partition will be replicated. If you install only one server in that partition, there will be only the Master replica of the partition. To ensure the root partition is replicated, you need to either install another server at the same context, or replicate it with one of the partition management utilities.

2. If you design a wide, flat tree with numerous OUs below a single O container, the root server holds the Master replica of the root partition, plus Read/Write replicas of *all* partitions below it. Keeping that many replicas in synchronization could impact the performance of the root server.

Partition Distribution

When considering partition distribution, remember the two purposes of partition replicas:

1. Partition replicas provide Directory fault tolerance by minimizing the risk of any single point of failure for the Directory.

2. Partition replicas provide faster access to information for servers that are physically distant from the Master replica (usually across a WAN link).

Directory fault tolerance can be as simple as storing replicas of Directory partitions on different servers. The network performance issue involves efficiently placing replicas so information accessed from servers in different physical locations does not cause excess network traffic. To plan for this, you must consider how your users access resources and information from different parts of the Directory tree.

Small networks probably won't need to provide Directory information to users across a WAN link. Your main concern when planning Directory replication is to provide fault tolerance for the Directory database to eliminate (or at least reduce) any single point of failure on the network. This can be accomplished by merely distributing replicas of Directory partitions on two or more servers.

On larger networks where some users need access to Directory information across a WAN link, you must consider both Directory fault tolerance (to eliminate or reduce the chance for any single point of failure on the network) *and* performance issues to make the Directory more responsive to users.

Providing fault tolerance for the Directory

Any time more than one server is installed in a container object, you have Directory fault tolerance (by default). This is because a Master replica is automatically placed on the first server installed in a container object, and all subsequent servers added to that container receive a Read/Write replica.

After installing a server in your Directory tree, you should check to see whether the partition is replicated as you expected. If not, you can replicate it and place it manually using the NetWare utilities. You can store a replica of one partition along with a replica of another partition on the same server.

N O T E There must be *at least two* replicas of every Directory partition on the network so you can restore the partition if anything should happen to it. If you lost a partition and did not have a replica of that partition, you could permanently lose access to the part of your Directory tree covered by that partition.

Figure 4-4 shows an example of the *maximum* amount of replication and distribution possible for a simple four-server network. In a production environment, this would probably be too much replication, but this example illustrates the concept.

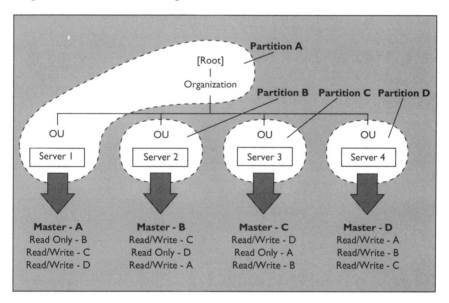

Figure 4-4. Example of the maximum Directory fault tolerance for a simple four-server network.

On actual networks, we recommend you have at least three copies of each Directory partition. For disaster recovery purposes, consider storing an additional copy of each Directory partition on an off-site server.

While you can have an unlimited number of replicas of each Directory partition, you should never need more than eight to 10 replicas of any partition. Remember, the more replicas you have, the more network traffic is generated during replica updates. In small networks, try not to place more than five replicas on any one server.

Another important point to consider when planning partitioning and replication is how much information you need (or want) in each of your partitions. The only limitation on the size of a replica is the amount of physical disk space on the server that stores the replica. Since disk space is a valuable resource, you should avoid unnecessary replication and keep the size of your replicas reasonable.

If one or more of your Directory partitions becomes larger than you want, or if you have a large partition and need to replicate only part of it, you can use the NetWare 4 partition management utilities (the Partition Manager tool in the NWAdmin graphical utility or the PARTMGR text utility) to split the partition into a more manageable size. For information on these utilities and their use, refer to Chapter 13.

Providing faster access to Directory information

If you have users who need to access Directory information across a WAN link, you should consider placing a replica of the necessary partition(s) on one of the user's local servers. Because most Directory information is accessed for informational purposes and is more likely to be read than modified, you can usually decrease network traffic (in this case WAN traffic) by placing any heavily accessed partition replicas on the local server. Remember, network traffic still is generated during replica synchronization (to update the database).

Figure 4-5 shows an example of a possible replica distribution scheme for the Widgetco tree.

Note the following points about this replication example:

- Servers at each site store Master replicas of the local partitions. The server at the corporate headquarters in Cody,

Wyoming, stores the Master replica of Widgetco (the root partition). A server at the Washington, D.C., office stores a Master replica of Sales-East. A server in Phoenix, Arizona, stores the Master replica of Sales-West.

- To make the Directory information for the remote offices locally accessible to users at the corporate headquarters, servers at the Cody, Wyoming, location store Read/Write replicas of Sales-East and Sales-West.

- To allow the sales people in Phoenix, Arizona, to access Directory information about their counterparts in the Washington, D.C., office without having to use a WAN link, a server in Phoenix stores a replica of Sales-East.

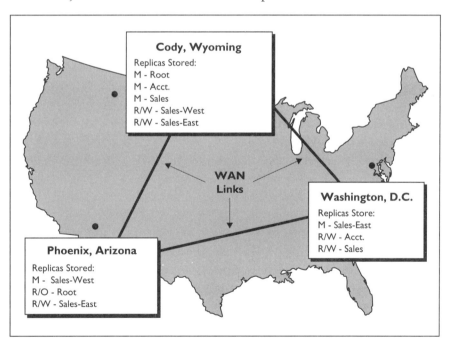

Cody, Wyoming
Replicas Stored:
M - Root
M - Acct.
M - Sales
R/W - Sales-West
R/W - Sales-East

WAN Links

Washington, D.C.
Replicas Store:
M - Sales-East
R/W - Acct.
R/W - Sales

Phoenix, Arizona
Replicas Stored:
M - Sales-West
R/O - Root
R/W - Sales-East

Figure 4-5. Example of distributing replicas around the network for Directory fault tolerance and efficient access.

This is only one example of using replicas to provide efficient access and fault tolerance. Since you know your network environment and business needs, you must decide the best method of replicating your Directory partitions and distributing the replicas across your network.

Carefully weigh which option is more efficient for your network: accessing Directory information across a WAN link, or placing a copy of the replica on the local server (but generating network traffic during updates). Also consider whether you have enough disk space on the local server to hold the necessary replica or replicas.

Before distributing replicas of Directory partitions, decide exactly how much information you need in each partition. Because replicas are physical entities that are stored on servers, unnecessary information stored in a replica can be a waste of disk space. Remember, NetWare 4 allows you to split a partition if it becomes overly large.

Summary

This chapter has provided an explanation of Directory partitions and replicas, and how NetWare 4's defaults are designed to provide a basic distribution of the NDS database across the network. Use the information in this chapter to efficiently plan replication so users have fast access to NDS information, according to the physical layout of your network. Be sure your plan also provides adequate Directory fault tolerance for your network with as little impact as possible on network traffic.

This chapter also mentioned the utilities that can be used to manage and change Directory partitions and replicas. The use of these utilities are covered in Chapter 13.

CHAPTER

5

NDS Time Synchronization

NetWare Directory Services relies heavily on a new feature in NetWare 4 called *time synchronization*. This new service ensures accuracy in the Directory database by making sure changes are updated in the proper order. To keep time consistent across the network, certain servers are set up as "time source" servers. Other servers read the time from these sources and synchronize their internal clocks as necessary.

This chapter gives an overview of time synchronization services and explains the importance of time stamps for NDS events. It introduces the four types of Time Servers and gives some configuration guidelines for various network needs. This information should help you formulate a time synchronization plan for your Directory tree.

Why Time Synchronization?

In NetWare 4, the main purpose of time synchronization is to maintain the same "universal" time on all servers. Servers must agree on a common time to ensure accuracy when changes are made to the Directory database. A secondary purpose of time synchronization is to provide the correct time of day. Accurate time can be fed into the network in several ways, discussed later in this chapter.

The importance of time stamps

Because the NDS database is distributed globally, any changes made to the database are first written to the local writable replica of the database. Once the change is written to the local replica, it is propagated to the other replicas of the database around the network.

Whenever an event occurs that affects the Directory (such as a new object being created, an object being renamed, or a password being changed), NDS requests a time stamp. A *time stamp* is a unique code consisting of both the exact date and time the event took place and the identity of the replica that initiated the event. Time stamps log the order in which the events occurred, and, thus, the proper order in which they should be replicated.

While it may not seem important to make changes in strict chronological order, it is critical to proper Directory synchronization and accurate Directory information. For instance, there is a big difference between deleting an object and then recreating it, versus creating an object and then deleting it.

In cases where an object is modified twice on the local replica, or simultaneously modified on two different replicas, there could be problems with conflicting information when the changes are propagated to the various replicas around the network. Without time stamps to know the order in which the changes actually were made, NDS would have no idea how to resolve such conflicts.

Universal time standard

Because of the global capabilities of NetWare 4, a network may have servers in various locations throughout the world, and, thus, in different time zones. To provide a "universal" common ground, time synchronization services are designed to key off Universal Time Coordinated (UTC) time. This is the worldwide time standard coordinated to the zero meridian (0° of longitude), or what used to be known as Greenwich Mean Time. No matter where in the world a particular server is located, its time is set according to UTC time.

With UTC as the time standard for the network, all time stamps are based on the same time. That way, the time stamps for any events that take place anywhere on the network are properly ordered and timed on the same basis, independent of the location of NDS replicas.

At first, it may seem like a big hassle to coordinate all servers in a global network to a standard time. But with time synchronization, the system is actually quite simple and effective. When set up properly, your network has access to time synchronization services to produce time stamps based on UTC time regardless of where servers are located. The Directory does not care what time zone any servers or replicas reside in, as long as there is one single basis used for time stamps across the network.

During the NetWare 4 installation process, each server is set according to how much its local time differs from UTC time. For instance, if I were setting up a Time Server in New York City, another one in Chicago, and a third in San Francisco, I would indicate during the installation how much each server's local time was ahead of UTC through the use of offsets. A *time offset* is the amount of time that must be *added* to the local time in order to convert local time to current UTC time.

Time offsets are usually set in hours and are positive values for all locations west of the zero meridian and negative values for all locations east of the zero meridian. For the New York City server, the time offset is +5, since the local time in New York (Eastern Standard Time) is five hours

79

behind the time in Greenwich, England. In other words, you must add five hours to New York local time to get Greenwich time.

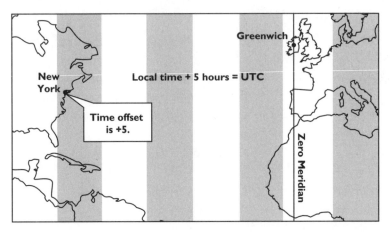

Figure 5-1. The time offset indicates how much time must be added to local time to convert it to UTC time.

For areas that switch to daylight savings time for part of the year, you can also configure servers to automatically compensate for the time changes. More information on the configuration parameters for time synchronization is given in Chapter 9.

Types of Time Servers

When you install a NetWare 4 server, you may designate the type of time server you want. To propagate a common time across the network, NetWare employs a combination of four distinct types of time servers:

1. Secondary Time Server (STS)

2. Primary Time Server (PTS)

3. Reference Time Server (RTS)

4. Single Reference Time Server (SRTS)

These represent different ways in which NetWare 4 servers can be configured for time synchronization. Each type of Time Server performs a particular function.

Secondary Time Server

A Secondary Time Server (STS) obtains the network time from one of the other three types of Time Servers (a Single Reference, Reference, or Primary Time Server). It can then provide that time to clients, such as workstations or applications.

A Secondary Time Server is not considered a "time source" server. It does not participate with other servers in the voting process to determine the correct network time. It simply accepts the time it receives and adjusts its internal clock accordingly.

Primary Time Server

A Primary Time Server (PTS) synchronizes network time with at least one other Primary or Reference Time Server. As a time source, it provides the time to Secondary Time Servers and to clients.

A PTS polls other time source servers (Primary or Reference Time Servers) to see what time they have, and then votes with these servers to determine network time. Once a common network time is decided on, the Primary Time Servers adjust their internal clocks to synchronize with that time.

Because all Primary Time Servers adjust their clocks to synchronize network time, network time can drift slightly if there are only Primary and Secondary Time Servers on the network.

Reference Time Server

A Reference Time Server (RTS) provides a time to which all other Time Servers and clients can synchronize. An RTS polls other Primary or

81

Reference Time Servers, then votes with them to synchronize the time. Unlike a PTS, a Reference Time Server does not change its clock after this polling process. This forces Primary Time Servers to reach a consensus on the correct network time based on the time provided by the Reference server.

An RTS provides a central point of control for network time. To prevent time drift, it is recommended that a Reference Time Server be synchronized with an external time source. Depending on the degree of accuracy required, this external source can be a radio clock or modem connection that receives time signals from the U.S. Naval Observatory or some other accurate time-keeping source. It may also be as simple as the network supervisor reading the time from a wall clock or wrist watch. Of course, the more accurate the time source is, the more efficient your Directory synchronization will be.

Single Reference Time Server

The Single Reference Time Server (SRTS) is a special case of the Reference Time Server. The main difference is that, as the name implies, the SRTS is the sole source of time for the entire network. The network supervisor sets the time on the Single Reference Time Server and this time becomes the correct network time.

When using the Single Reference Time Server, you cannot have any Primary or Reference Time Servers on the network. All other servers must be configured as Secondary Time Servers that get their time from the SRTS.

NOTE

Because the Single Reference Time Server is the sole source of time on the network on which it is installed, all other servers on the network must be able to contact it.

In summary, Single Reference, Reference, and Primary Time Servers are all considered to be time source servers. Time source servers provide time to other servers and clients. Secondary Time Servers do not provide time to the network, and, thus, are not considered time source servers. Secondary Time Servers only receive the correct network time from a time source server and pass this correct time on to clients.

Time Server Configuration Methods

The question arises as to how Time Servers "find" each other on the network. This process can be configured in two different ways: by using NetWare's Service Advertising Protocol (SAP), or through a custom configuration process. Both methods provide the necessary contact for time synchronization, but they achieve the desired result in different ways.

Each configuration has advantages and disadvantages you should consider in light of how you are implementing and using your network.

Service Advertising Protocol method

By default, all Single Reference, Reference, and Primary Time Servers use NetWare's Service Advertising Protocol (SAP) to announce their presence on the network. However, the different types of servers use SAP in the following ways:

- Primary and Reference Time Servers use SAP information to find other servers to poll for determining the network time.

- Secondary Time Servers use SAP information to find and choose a time server from which to get the network time.

The main advantage of the SAP method is it allows for easy installation without having to worry about the physical layout of your network. This method also allows you to quickly and efficiently reconfigure time synchronization services when operating modes are changed or when you add new Time Servers to your network.

As a possible disadvantage, the SAP method generates additional network traffic. The larger the network is, the more SAP traffic is generated on the network by Time Server SAP broadcasts. When time synchronization first begins, polling between servers occurs every 10 seconds. As the network time stabilizes, the polling interval gradually increases to once every 10 minutes. When servers reach a stable state, the amount of traffic attributable to time synchronization is very small compared to normal network traffic.

Time synchronization traffic can create problems in network environments where "test" servers are brought up and down frequently. This is especially true if these servers are configured as a time sources (Single Reference, Reference, or Primary Time Servers). The frequent addition and removal of extra servers in the time-polling loop may cause disruptions of the network time and lead to synchronization problems.

When the SAP method is used for time synchronization, be careful when setting the time on a server you intend to bring up as a time source. *Never set a time source server to a time in the* future! If you do, it could throw off network time to the point where the NDS database will not accept any updates. If anything, you should set the new server's clock a minute or so *behind* the network synchronized time.

The custom configuration method provides some protection against a situation such as this accidentally taking place

Custom configuration method

With the custom configuration method, you can assign which time source servers each server should contact for time information or polling. In addition, you can restrict a specified server from listening for SAP information from other time source servers, and you can restrict Time Servers from advertising their presence using SAP broadcasts.

The main advantage of custom configuration is it gives the network administrator complete control over the network time synchronization environment. You can eliminate nonessential SAP traffic and avoid errors associated with accidental synchronization with a new or "test" server. You may also distribute time sources around the network to optimize time-related traffic.

On the downside, however, the custom configuration method requires more planning and implementation time. Installation and removal of time source servers is more involved, as you must manually change the approved server list maintained in a configuration file on each server.

Time Synchronization Setup Considerations

Time synchronization is enabled during the NetWare 4 installation process. You first specify which type of Time Server you want the server to be. You then specify the time zone in which the server resides, as well as the Daylight Savings Time rules for the server.

In many cases, you can safely choose the NetWare defaults. The defaults provide a simple time-synchronization model that should be adequate in most small networks and in some medium-sized networks. However, the default setup is not necessarily the best, especially as the physical size of the network increases.

The following sections describe the default time-synchronization configuration, along with some alternate configurations that are more practical for certain types of networks.

Default time server configuration

The default configuration provided during installation of NetWare 4 is to make the first server installed a Single Reference Time Server, and all subsequent servers Secondary Time Servers. Also by default, Secondary Time Servers use the Service Advertising Protocol (SAP) to contact the time-source server.

The default setup can be used for networks of any size. However, this configuration is primarily recommended for use on small networks. It is easy to understand and requires no advance planning. Since there is no need to provide a configuration file, the default configuration is easier to manage in a small network environment.

Figure 5-2 shows an example of the default (recommended) time synchronization setup for a small network, using a Single Reference and Secondary Time Servers.

Remember, when you have a Single Reference Time Server, you cannot have any Reference or Primary Time Servers on the same network. Because the Single Reference Time Server is the *sole* source of time on the network, it is installed on, *all other servers* on the network must be able to contact it.

Set up your physical network topology so all servers are connected without intervening routers or slow, heavily used segments. If this is not possible, try to set it up so no Secondary Time Server is more than one hop away from the Single Reference server. This prevents an overabundance of network traffic caused by time-synchronization services.

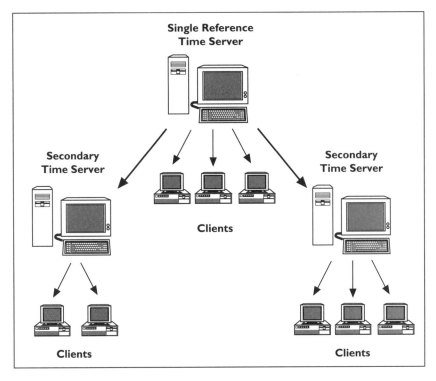

Figure 5-2. Example of a small network using Single Reference and Secondary Time Servers (default configuration).

Alternate configurations

One drawback of the default configuration is that with only one time source, there is a single source of failure. If the Single Reference Time Server goes down, the network is without a source of time. Also, the physical topology of larger networks sometimes dictates that there be several time sources distributed throughout the network.

If your network needs dictate that you use a time-synchronization setup other than the default, the recommended alternate configuration is to replace the Single Reference Time Server with Reference and Primary Time Servers.

87

On a small network, try to have no more than one Reference Time Server. Since a Reference Time Server needs at least one other time source server to poll, you should also install a Primary Time Server somewhere on the same network. You could install another Reference Time Server instead, but this is discouraged for small networks, as it usually causes more traffic with no additional benefit.

NOTE Remember, whenever Reference and Primary servers are used on a network, they must all be able to "see" each other. Secondary servers must always be able to see at least one time source (Primary, Reference, or Single Reference Time Server).

On medium-sized networks, using a Reference Time Server with Primary Time Servers provides the best performance. We recommend you use this configuration unless circumstances strongly dictate otherwise, as in Figure 5-3.

To use an external time source, the Reference Time Server's hardware clock option must be turned off during the installation process. Several third-party products are available to set a server's time from external sources, such as a radio clock or modem device. Some examples are listed in Appendix B.

TIP In the absence of an external time source, you can turn on the hardware clock option as a kind of cheap substitute. This causes a Reference server to set time from its own internal hardware clock during each polling loop.

On large, geographically dispersed networks, use multiple time-source servers to provide local access and reduce overall network traffic. For instance, it might be useful to have a Reference Time Server at each location accessed across a WAN link (where the location also has several Primary Time Servers). By locating an RTS at each of these sites, you eliminate the need for Primary servers to poll Reference Time Servers across the WAN link and generate nonproductive, yet necessary, "time" traffic across the WAN link.

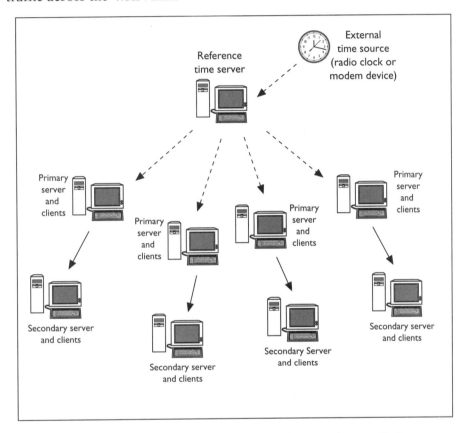

Figure 5-3. Example of a medium-sized network using Reference and Primary Time Servers.

Whenever you have more than one Reference server on the network, each Reference server must be individually synchronized through an external time source. Two Reference servers will not synchronize with each other.

Primary Time Servers are designed for use on larger networks to increase fault tolerance by providing redundant paths for Secondary Time Servers.

If one Primary Time Server goes down, the Secondary Time Server can still get the network time from an alternate Primary Time Server. On a large network, I recommend you use at least one Primary Time Server for every 125 to 150 Secondary Time Servers.

Finally, Secondary Time Servers *can* contact other Secondary Time Servers to get the time if absolutely necessary. However, this situation should be avoided as it adds another level of potential synchronization error.

When to use custom configuration

On small networks, consider using the custom configuration in the following situations:

- Where there is frequent reconfiguration, such as when servers are constantly added or removed.

- When you expect your network to grow rapidly in the short term.

If your network is in a growth situation, using the custom configuration now can help you avoid growing pains later. You will have more control over future time synchronization, as well as over future network performance.

While you can use a combination of the SAP and custom configuration methods on the same network, it is usually best to disable the use of SAP altogether if you're doing a custom configuration. In cases where both the SAP and custom configurations are used, the custom configuration information stored on a server always takes precedence over any SAP information received by the server.

Time Synchronization Guidelines

To implement an effective time-synchronization plan for your network, consider the topology and time synchronization needs of your network and decide the following:

- How many Time Servers do you really need?

- What type of Time Server will each of these servers be?

- Where will time source servers be located to provide effective fault tolerance and to minimize network traffic generated by Time Servers?

The best time-synchronization setups for NDS are those that are the simplest. We often get caught up in the "more is better" mentality. But in the case of NetWare time synchronization, less is usually better and more efficient.

Here are some guidelines for keeping your time synchronization setup simple:

- If you have a Single Reference Time Server on your network, designate all other servers on the network as Secondary Time Servers.

- In a nondefault configuration, keep the number of Reference and Primary Time Servers on your network to as few as you can get by with comfortably.

- Once all of the necessary time source servers (Primary and Reference) are designated on your network, designate all other network servers as Secondary Time Servers. Servers will be designated as Secondary servers by default for all but the first server installed on the network.

- A Secondary server must always be able to see at least one time source (Primary, Reference, or Single Reference Time Server) to adjust its clock.

- For optimal performance, set up Secondary Time Servers to contact time source servers that are physically close. This reduces overall network "time" traffic. Avoid placing Secondary Time Servers more than one hop away from a time source server. Direct connections with no intervening routers or slow segments are preferred, whenever possible.

- In some instances, Secondary Time Servers can be the most efficient way of providing time to other Secondary Time Servers. However, this may add one more level of potential synchronization error.

- When Reference and Primary servers are used together, they must all be able to see each other.

- You should rarely need more than one Reference Time Server on a small network. However, if you have a distant location with several servers and this location does not have a constant direct line to the rest of your WAN, you may decide to place an additional Reference Time Server there to take care of local time synchronization.

  Every network that includes a Reference Time Server must also include at least one of the following time source servers on the same network: a Primary Time Server (recommended) or another Reference Time Server.

- If your network includes more than one Reference server, remember each must be synchronized through an external time source. Various third-party products are available to provide external time source synchronization (see Appendix B).

After choosing the proper time-synchronization configuration for your network, inform all who will install NetWare 4 on servers on the network. This will help them assign the correct time-synchronization function on each server they install.

Summary

Time synchronization is critical to the proper synchronization of the Directory database in NDS. While it seems complicated, the best time-synchronization setups for NDS are those that are the simplest. Carefully consider how you network is configured, as well as how the network will be used before setting up your network time synchronization.

With the information provided in this chapter, you should be able to efficiently plan a time-synchronization setup for your network. Remember not to get too caught up in the perceived complexity. Rather, consider the usefulness and efficiency this feature can provide for your network.

Netware Bindery Emulation

O ne of the least-touted features of NetWare 4 is bindery emulation. Despite all the attention given to the new Directory
Services, most applications and services that run in the NetWare
environment do not currently take full advantage of the NDS feature set.
Novell provides bindery emulation to enable users of these services to
access them in the NetWare 4 environment.

This chapter provides an overview of bindery emulation, its uses, and its
limitations. The information is designed to help network administrators
configure their NetWare 4 network environments so that bindery-based
clients can still access resources on a NetWare 4 network.

Compatibility with Bindery-Based NetWare

In NetWare versions 2 and 3, all network objects (users, printers, and so on) were defined on a single server in a flat database known as the "bindery." Any network user who was logged in to a server and had the appropriate NetWare rights was permitted access to the services bound to that server.

Each individual server was responsible for maintaining its own bindery information about the users, groups, print queues, and so on that resided on that server. For example, the bindery contained various bits of information about a user such as the user's name, object ID, password, and security equivalences. If one user logged in to several different servers, he or she would have unique information on each of those servers.

Figure 6-1 shows a typical NetWare bindery in NetWare versions prior to NetWare 4.

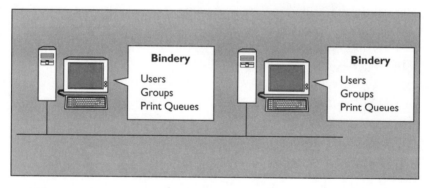

Figure 6-1. In previous versions of NetWare, the bindery held all of the information about a server's users, groups, print queues, and so on.

Bindery-based file servers did not share bindery information with one another. Each server had its own bindery, and, thus, each server had to be maintained and administered separately, which often became burdensome in larger networks.

In NetWare 4, the use of binderies is eliminated in favor of a hierarchical Directory structure consisting of containers and their respective objects. NDS uses Organization (O) and Organizational Unit (OU) containers to organize all of the objects in the Directory database in a logical manner. Objects organized in these containers include users, servers, queues, and other network entities and services. The information in the NDS database is then shared among servers throughout the network.

Figure 6-2 shows a typical hierarchical Directory tree.

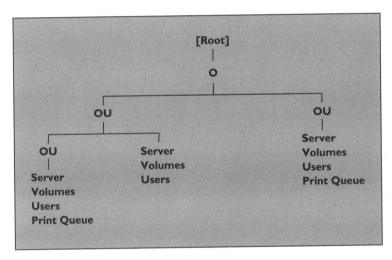

Figure 6-2. Instead of individual server binderies, NDS uses a global database implemented in a hierarchical tree structure.

By replacing the server-specific bindery with a more useful network-wide database, NDS enables clients to login to the network. Once logged in and authenticated, clients can access any areas of the Directory for which they have the proper access rights.

NetWare Directory Services was designed to provide easier access to network services and to simplify network administration. As we have seen, this design allows for more sophisticated and productive networks, while easing the problems of network administration that were previously associated with large networks.

Why bindery emulation?

Most companies tend to upgrade their networks in incremental steps, rather than all at once. There is usually a period of time during which new versions and older versions of NetWare overlap. Recognizing this, Novell designed bindery emulation to provide backward compatibility between NetWare 4 and various bindery-based services and utilities that might need to coexist with NetWare 4. In addition to many third-party utilities that are bindery-based, the list of services that require bindery emulation includes current versions of Novell's own NetWare for Macintosh, NetWare for SAA, and NetWare NFS products. Future versions of these products will fully support NDS.

Of course, another reason for bindery emulation is to allow existing bindery-based clients (defined on NetWare 2 and 3 servers) to login to NetWare 4 servers and access some of their resources during a transitionary period. NetWare 4 comes with new DOS client software called the NetWare DOS Requester or Virtual Loadable Modules (VLMs). This is the same "universal" client software that ships with NetWare 3.12 (the latest release in the NetWare 3 family). Installing the new VLMs on all DOS clients simplifies both the coexistence period and the actual upgrade to NetWare 4. (The VLM client software is discussed in detail in Chapter 10).

Through the use of NetWare bindery emulation, both users and programs are able to access many NDS objects just as they accessed bindery objects in previous NetWare versions. With a little planning, your network's bindery-based users can take at least partial advantage of the NetWare 4 Directory.

How bindery emulation works

When bindery emulation is enabled, NDS imitates a flat structure for all leaf objects in a single container object (an Organization or Organizational Unit). This allows objects in a specified container to be accessed by bindery-based clients and servers, as well as by NDS objects. Bindery emulation applies only to *leaf* objects that are not NDS-specific. These objects would include User, Group, Print Server, and Print Queue objects.

Each NetWare 4 server has a *bindery context,* which is a pointer to the container object where bindery emulation is set. The bindery context can be set or changed by using the SET BINDERY CONTEXT= server command with the proper parameters.

When a new server is installed into the Directory tree, NetWare 4 automatically creates a server object in the specified container object. By default, the NetWare 4 installation process enables bindery emulation on the server and sets the bindery context automatically.

For bindery emulation to work, a Read/Write replica of the partition containing the correct bindery context must be located on each server on which you want bindery emulation enabled. The NetWare 4 installation process places this necessary Read/Write replica by default whenever a new server is installed into an existing context. Whenever a new server is installed into a new context, a Master replica is placed on that server (by default).

Figure 6-3 illustrates how bindery emulation works in a Directory tree where the bindery context is enabled on an Organizational Unit object.

With bindery emulation, bindery-based clients still login to a specific server rather than the network. The clients can only see the leaf objects that exist in the container (O or OU) to which that server's bindery context points.

Different NetWare 4 servers can have different bindery contexts. However, bindery-emulation users only have access to objects that reside in the specified bindery context for the server to which they login.

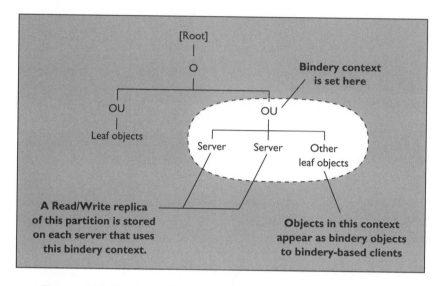

Figure 6-3. For bindery emulation to work, you need a bindery context set and a Read/Write or Master replica on each server.

It is important to understand that bindery emulation is server centric. Because NDS is emulating a flat bindery, the login process for bindery-emulation users is the same as for previous versions of NetWare. In other words, a DOS client doing a bindery login must have a login script that resides in the user's MAIL directory on the server to which the user is logging in. Changes a user makes to his or her bindery login script are not propagated to other servers on the network, whereas an NDS client's login information would be.

However, there is a significant difference between an emulated bindery under NetWare 4 and the actual bindery in NetWare 2 and 3. Bindery-based servers do not share information, whereas *all* NetWare 4 servers that reside in the same Directory tree (including those running bindery emulation) share the information in the Directory. If you use bindery emulation, any operation performed on one server's bindery affects any other servers that exist in the same bindery context. For example, if changes are made to a Directory object, such a changing a user object's rights, those changes are replicated across the network and affect the entire Directory.

Bindery Emulation Setup Considerations

This section outlines several issues to consider while planning your bindery emulation implementation.

User naming rules

When planning for bindery emulation, keep in mind that the names you give to NDS objects must conform to the naming rules for bindery-based objects. These naming rules are:

- Bindery emulation object names can contain up to 47 characters.

- Bindery emulation object names cannot contain spaces, slashes, backslashes, colons, semicolons, commas, asterisks, square brackets, angle brackets, vertical bars, plus signs, equal signs, or question marks.

By keeping the naming of bindery emulation objects consistent, the objects appear the same to both NDS clients and non-NDS clients.

GUEST, EVERYONE, and SUPERVISOR

In bindery-based versions of NetWare, users GUEST and SUPERVISOR, and group EVERYONE were automatically created. This is not the case in NetWare 4:

- The user object GUEST is not automatically created in NetWare 4 bindery emulation. If you need a user GUEST or if you use a service that requires the user GUEST, you must manually create the GUEST User object.

101

- NetWare 4 bindery emulation does not create the group object EVERYONE automatically. Again, if you use a service (such as NetWare NFS) that requires the group EVERYONE, you must manually create the group and add users to the group.

- The bindery user object SUPERVISOR is not automatically created, nor is it used under Directory Services. However, you can create a SUPERVISOR User object and assign Admin-equivalent rights to this user. In NetWare 4, the user SUPERVISOR *does* exist as a bindery-emulation user object. Although it is not visible under NDS, the SUPERVISOR user object can be accessed through a bindery emulation login.

When *upgrading* from NetWare 3 to NetWare 4, all bindery users and groups are converted to Directory objects. The user SUPERVISOR is converted, but without the supervisory rights associated with it in NetWare 3.

Accessible information

Bindery emulation can only access information that has a counterpart in the actual bindery. Bindery-based users cannot access NDS information that is not also found in a bindery, such as:

- E-mail name

- Phone number

- Print job configurations

- Aliases

The inability to access this NDS-specific information is not usually a problem for bindery-emulation users. It does underscore the usefulness of the Directory and the information it contains, and, thus, provides another valid reason for upgrading your network to all NetWare 4 servers with NDS clients as quickly as possible.

Partitioning limitation

In NetWare 4, a server's bindery context can only be set to a container stored on that specific server. This means the server must hold either a Master replica or a Read/Write replica that includes the container in which the server is located. In other words, the bindery context can only be set to a container included in a writable NDS replica.

When you use the NetWare 4 default partition management scheme, a writable replica is created automatically on the proper server. If you are not using the defaults, such a replica must be created manually.

Examples of Bindery Contexts

Bindery-emulation clients (including various services) are limited to working with only those servers and objects located in their specific bindery context. Remember, the bindery context is simply a pointer that indicates which NDS container unit holds the bindery emulation objects. Bindery-emulation limits each server to only one bindery context.

While you can set the bindery context from the command line at the server, the easiest way is to include the "SET BINDERY CONTEXT=*Context*" command in the AUTOEXEC.NCF file on each server.

Single bindery context

If you use a simple, flat Directory structure that contains only one level, there can be only one possible bindery context. Figure 6-4 shows a flat NDS tree structure with only one level (an O container).

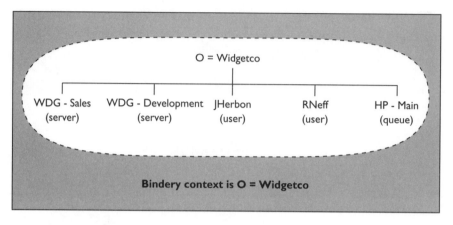

Figure 6-4. In a flat NDS tree structure with one container, there is only one possible bindery context.

In this figure, the NDS structure is exactly like that of a traditional bindery. Because the tree only has one container object, the bindery context for servers WDG-Sales and WDG-Development would be set to O=Widgetco. This would be accomplished by adding the following command to each of the server's AUTOEXEC.NCF files:

```
set bindery context=o=widgetco
```

All users located in the container object O=Widgetco are able to login to either of the servers under bindery emulation. For example, in Figure 6-4 bindery emulation users JHERBON and RNEFF can log in to either of the servers shown.

Multiple bindery contexts

In most circumstances, the Directory tree hierarchy contains more than one level. The bindery context thus has a more noticeable effect on the bindery emulation users' ability to access services and resources on the network. Consider the NDS tree structure shown in Figure 6-5.

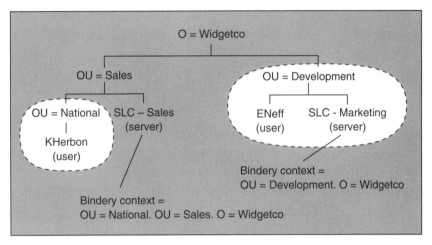

Figure 6-5. Two different bindery contexts in the same Directory tree.

This tree has four container objects, listed below with their complete names:

1. O=Widgetco

2. OU=Sales.O=Widgetco

3. OU=Development.O=Widgetco

4. OU=National.OU=Sales.O=Widgetco

You can set a server's bindery context to *any* Organizational Unit (OU) or Organization (O) included in a writable replica that resides on that specific server. Thus, given the partitions shown in Figure 6-5, the bindery context of SLC-Sales could be set to any of the following containers:

- **OU=Sales.** This is the default location for server SLC-Sales.

- **OU=National.** By default, SLC-Sales would have a replica. However, if it were removed, the context could not be set here.

- **O=Widgetco.** Use this container only if some "privileged" user added a replica of the O=Widgetco partition, since the replica would not reside on SLC-Sales by default.)

- **OU=Development.** Use this container only if the partition is manually copied to SLC-Sales.

By default, a server's bindery context is set to the container object that holds the server. The server's bindery context can be changed from the default by changing the SET BINDERY CONTEXT= line in the server's AUTOEXEC.NCF file. NetWare 4 also allows you to change the bindery context at the server's console prompt by typing **SET BINDERY CON-TEXT=***new context.*

Whenever you set or change the bindery context, begin with the name of the container object to which you want to set the new context, and then work your way up the tree. If you needed to set the bindery context for server SLC-Sales in Figure 6-5 to OU=Sales so users in that OU can login to that server, put the following command in that server's AUTOEXEC.NCF file:

```
SET BINDERY CONTEXT=OU=Sales.O=Widgetco
```

This command sets the bindery context to the OU=Sales container and provides the correct path for NDS to use in finding that container.

If your tree is relatively small (similar to the one in Figure 6-5), you might want to simplify it by having only one partition. If you only have one partition, you could set the bindery context to any OU or O in the Directory tree.

Be sure of how you want to set up your servers' bindery contexts before implementing bindery emulation. Once in place, a bindery context should not be changed, as that would prevent all bindery emulation users who were using the original context to login to that server from accessing the network. Changing a server's bindery context can also prevent bindery emulation users' access to network print queues.

In the example shown in Figure 6-5, SLC-Sales is the only server to which KHERBON can login. Likewise, the only server on which ENEFF can login is SLC-Marketing. These users are limited to these servers because the servers have their bindery context set to the location of those user objects. If either server's bindery context were changed, these bindery-emulation users would be unable to login to the changed servers. For example, if the bindery context of SLC-Sales was changed to O=Widgetco, KHERBON cannot login because the server's bindery context no longer points to the container which holds user KHERBON.

Accessing different servers in the same bindery context

There are times when a bindery emulation user on a NetWare 4 network needs access to more than one server. If any of your users need to access several servers, plan your network in such a way that you can use the same bindery context for all of those servers. An easy way to achieve this is to locate the server objects in the same container that holds the user objects that need this access are located in. Figure 6-6 shows an example of this structure.

In Figure 6-6, user ENEFF can access both servers within the OU=Accounting bindery context (PRV-Receivable and PRV-Payable). However, if the bindery context of either server was changed, ENEFF would be unable to login to the changed server.

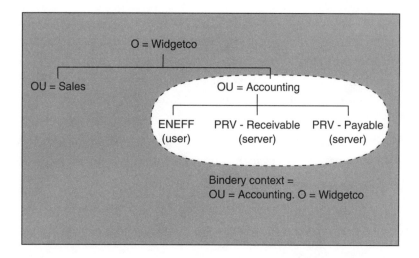

Figure 6-6. Example of several servers that can be accessed in the same bindery context.

You might find that it isn't possible or practical to locate all of the servers that are used by your bindery-emulation users in the same container as those users. In this situation, ensure that all of the servers who need to have the same bindery context hold a writable replica of the partition that contains the Organizational Unit to which you want the bindery context set.

Through its partition and replica management features, NetWare 4 allows you the flexibility to designate and place replicas where you need them. This built-in flexibility makes it simple and manageable to place multiple servers in the same bindery context where needed by your bindery-emulation users. An example of this is shown in Figure 6-7.

In Figure 6-7, notice that both PRV-Sales and PRV-Marketing have their bindery context set to OU=Sales. Thus user KHERBON can login to both servers even though the servers are located in different places on the network. This is possible because both servers have the same bindery context.

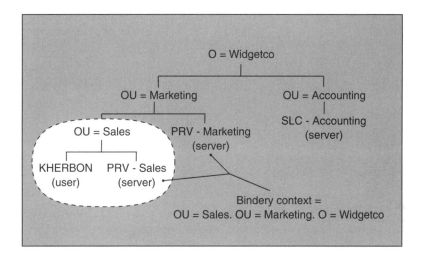

Figure 6-7. An example of multiple servers in different locations on the network with the same bindery context.

Accessing objects that reside in a different bindery context

While it is preferable that all objects accessed by a bindery-emulation user be located in the same bindery context as the user, there are times when this is neither possible nor practical. However, there is a way that a bindery-emulation user can access objects that reside outside the user's bindery context.

As in previous versions of bindery-based NetWare, bindery-emulation users must have a separate account on each server accessed by that user. NetWare 4 bindery emulation allows a user to access objects in any bindery context, provided the user has at least one account in that bindery context.

For example, in Figure 6-7 user object KHERBON cannot login to SLC-Accounting, because she is not located in the PRV-Accounting server's bindery context. However, by simply creating user object KHERBON in OU=Accounting, user KHERBON can access server PRV-Accounting, as in Figure 6-8.

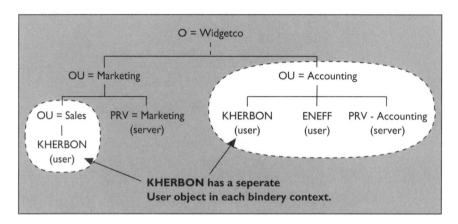

Figure 6-8. An example of creating multiple user objects for one person.

Note that NDS considers user KHERBON in OU=Sales and KHERBON in OU=Accounting to be two different entities. Bindery emulation does not require user objects to be identical in every bindery context where they are set up. It is quite likely that user KHERBON will not have the same rights on server PRV-Accounting that she has on server PRV-Marketing.

Just as in previous bindery-based versions of NetWare, the user's password and user name can be different in every bindery context. However, the user's life will be simpler if you use the same user name and password on all servers. If network security is important in your environment, it is better to use different user names and passwords to increase your basic network security.

For all of its benefits, bindery emulation is not a perfect solution. Its shortcomings become apparent in the areas of setting up and maintaining users. As in bindery-based versions of NetWare, whenever you set up accounts for a user on more than one server, that user must be granted appropriate rights to any and all objects the user needs access to on that specific server. Any time a user is removed from the network, you must delete the user's accounts on every server the user accesses.

By contrast, in NDS a user is created once and given rights to all of the services and resources he or she needs to access, no matter where they are on the network. NDS also provides central network management that allows you to delete a user from the network once, not several times on various different servers.

Planning for Bindery Emulation

The transition from NetWare 2 or 3 to NetWare 4 is expected to be a gradual process. While bindery emulation allows mixed-environment networks to coexist, its use disables much of Directory Service's object management functionality. Our recommendation is to use bindery emulation only when absolutely necessary. Once you make the paradigm shift from bindery-based NetWare and realize the full functionality of NetWare 4, there is no good reason for delaying a total network upgrade.

When you plan your Directory structure, be sure to consider any clients or services that need to use bindery emulation. As much as possible, try to place the objects that bindery emulation users will use in the same bindery context (container). If you have geographically distant sites, it is better to group servers at various bindery contexts for the following reasons:

- Having a separate bindery context for each location allows local control over the servers at each site. Local administrators can make Directory changes such as adding or deleting users and installing new servers.

- If you had only one bindery context, administrators from remote sites would all have to have Admin rights to that container. This might lead to conflicts if two administrators try to make changes at the same time. It also adds a certain security risk should an unauthorized person gain access at one of the remote sites.

- If bindery-emulation users had to access a single bindery context across WAN links, network traffic would increase and could cause performance problems. It is better to place the bindery contexts locally to minimize the amount of Directory information that must travel across WAN links.

Bindery-emulation users can access objects in other parts of the Directory by having multiple accounts. However, this method adds unnecessary administrative work, especially if numerous users need multiple accounts. While it may not be possible to avoid this situation in all circumstances, a little planning can reduce the number of accounts your users need.

Always consider your bindery-emulation users before making any changes to the Directory. Even minimal changes in the Directory structure could prevent your bindery-emulation users from accessing the network or network resources or services.

Summary

This chapter explains what bindery emulation is and provides insight on how to effectively plan your Directory structure so bindery-emulation users can access network resources easily. By understanding the concepts provided here and implementing them, your network should allow efficient coexistence of NDS and bindery-emulation clients on your network, while somewhat easing network administration.

Bindery emulation should be used only as a transitional tool to provide network access to bindery-based clients until you can switch your entire network to NetWare 4 with all NDS clients. Once you administer a mixed-environment network, the great advantages of NetWare 4 become quite apparent.

Designing Your Directory Tree

The most important preparation for upgrading or installing NetWare 4 is planning your Directory tree. The structure of the Directory affects your network's security, accessibility, and auditability. A carefully thought-out Directory tree allows you to take full advantage of all of the features and performance of NetWare 4.

Planning and implementing the Directory tree is more involved than setting up the bindery in previous versions of NetWare. In bindery-based NetWare, you simply installed servers, added users, and granted rights to shared resources, using various NetWare utilities. Advance planning was helpful, but not critical. Setting up a NetWare 4 Directory tree is not difficult, but it does require some thoughtful planning. A properly planned Directory tree gives you better control of your network, enhances security, and makes administration easier. Users also appreciate the ease-of-use of a well planned Directory tree.

The six previous chapters have presented the main concepts you need to understand to design an effective Directory. This chapter ties together everything you have learned previously, providing guidelines and alternatives to consider for the differing needs of simple and complex network environments.

Directory Planning Overview

Every Directory tree should be designed in a manner that will satisfy four main objectives:

1. Allow users to easily access Directory information (such as network resources).

2. Simplify the administration and maintenance of your network.

3. Provide Directory fault tolerance for the entire network.

4. Decrease unnecessary traffic on the network.

In addition, you should consider any specific needs or problems that may be unique to your network. Analyze the way people work in your organization—who needs access to what information, where that information is located, and how often they access different resources or services.

In a global or corporate-wide network, planning is important and will take some time. But a successful Directory structure will pay great dividends in increased network security, more efficient network management, and easier use and better sharing of network resources. Future network costs can also be reduced because no radical reworking of the Directory will be necessary.

An important point to keep in mind is that there is no single "correct" way to design an effective Directory tree. Every network is unique and has different requirements. It is often useful to plan your Directory tree in several different ways. Although this may take more time, you can then weigh the advantages and disadvantages of the various plans and decide on the one that best suits your network's needs. For a large network, it is a good idea to get input from other departments or groups in your organization.

Following is a general procedure to follow when planning your Directory tree. Each item is cross-referenced to different sections in this chapter and other chapters in this book. This chapter focuses mainly on steps 2 and 3. For more detailed information about the other items, refer to the specified chapter in this book.

1. **Plan and create a NetWare Directory Services "Naming Standards" document for consistent object naming across the network.** To ease network administration and use, it is important to define and document consistent object and property naming standards to be used throughout your network. Your naming standards document should detail acceptable naming conventions for naming Directory containers and leaf objects (users, printers, servers, and so on). It should also specify which property values you will use for each NDS object (such as telephone numbers, addresses, and so on) for User objects. Distribute this document to all network administrators who are responsible for setting up or maintaining any portion of the Directory tree. You might also consider publishing a register of names so the people who create new objects can determine whether a name is already in use. (For an example of an NDS Naming Standards Document, see Appendix A.)

2. **Define your Directory tree based on the most logical structure for your company or organization.** The logical structure of an organization can be defined in many ways. For example, it could be based on an organizational chart, physical locations, or job functions. In some situations, Directory planning may be as simple as setting up the tree to be identical to the existing organizational charts. Large companies may need to consider organizational structure at several levels that may include divisions or subsidiaries, departments, or even small workgroups. While corporate organizational structure is important, you must also consider such things as the physical location of users and

resources. For some, a Directory tree that is crafted to follow job functions or the way work flows within the organization may be most useful.

Design the tree starting with the top level. Once you've decided on the top level, proceed down to the next level of the tree, and the next, and so on. NetWare 4 does not limit the number of levels your tree can have. However, the fewer levels in a tree, the more efficient your network administration and use will be. (See "Planning the Top Levels of the Directory Tree" later in this chapter.)

3. **Determine the best way to use specific NDS objects and properties to efficiently organize your Directory tree.** Do an inventory of everything that needs to be included in your Directory tree. Sort the various objects by physical location, and then try to locate objects near the users who will access them. This keeps data flowing in relatively small segments, rather than traveling across numerous routers and possibly contributing to network traffic congestion. (See "Placing Objects in the Directory Tree" later in this chapter.)

4. **Plan the security for your Directory tree.** An important consideration when planning your Directory tree is deciding how to best control access to the objects that reside in your Directory tree. There are several ways to provide security for the different parts of your Directory tree. Because of the way rights naturally flow down the tree, NDS allows you to use the hierarchical structure of the tree itself to control access to objects. You also have the option of creating Inherited Rights Filters (IRFs) to limit access rights at different levels of the tree to restrict rights to the specified object at that level of the tree. NetWare 4

even allows you to implement container-level security for objects in a container. (For more detailed information on NDS access control and security, see Chapter 3.)

5. **Plan for distributed replication of the partitions that will provide maximum performance and Directory fault tolerance.** Once your Directory structure is decided, consider how you will divide the Directory database into partitions based on logical boundaries. You can then place replicas of the partitions throughout the network to provide adequate Directory fault tolerance, allow quick user access, and reduce traffic over WAN links. (For more detailed information on partitions and replicas, see Chapter 4.)

6. **Plan your network time synchronization.** Time synchronization is another important consideration in setting up a NetWare 4 network that will use NDS. Planning network time synchronization includes deciding which time synchronization configuration is best for your network, and then designating the proper types of time servers in the proper locations to efficiently implement your chosen configuration. (For more detailed information about time synchronization, see Chapter 5.)

7. **If you will be using bindery emulation, provide for the needs of bindery emulation users and services.** Until more NetWare add-on services and third-party utilities are developed specifically for NDS, bindery emulation will be a fact of life. You should be aware of the special needs of bindery emulation as you plan your Directory tree. (For more detailed information about bindery emulation, see Chapter 6.)

8. **If you are upgrading servers from NetWare 2 or 3, develop a migration plan to prepare the servers.** There are several preparations you need to make before migrating an exist-

ing NetWare 2 or 3 server to NetWare 4. These steps include cleaning up the bindery and the file system, and backing up all file system data. You should also consider your network needs during the coexistence period when you will work with both NetWare 4 and previous versions of NetWare together. (For help in developing an upgrade and coexistence strategy, see Chapter 8.)

While NetWare 4 does provide utilities to manipulate your Directory once it is implemented, nothing can take the place of advance planning. Directory planning may not be totally painless, but in the long run, your network will experience easier and more efficient use and management through careful planning. The information and guidelines provided in this book should make it easier to accomplish this task. Refer to the planning chapters frequently while planning and designing your Directory tree.

Now it's time to start planning your tree. Good luck!

Designing the Structure of Your Directory Tree

In presenting ideas for structuring a Directory tree, this book considers a network's uses and needs rather than talking about arbitrarily defined network sizes. This way, you can make the choices that best fit your needs.

Using the defaults

The NetWare 4 installation defaults are designed to let you set up a simple tree with very little planning. If you use the defaults for your Directory tree, NetWare provides default leaf objects (such as User object Admin), simple Directory partitions, network time synchronization, and bindery emulation.

While this is certainly the quickest way to set up a network, it is not necessarily the best. This default installation doesn't take full advantage of NetWare Directory Services. Most advanced networks will benefit from using a customized Directory structure. To optimize your network for both users and administrators, you should take the time and implement a Directory tree that meets all of your network needs.

How many trees?

This is a question that many early NetWare 4 implementers seem to be struggling with. Some feel that it would be more practical to create several "departmental" trees and later merge them together to form the corporate-wide tree. However, designing and creating only one Directory tree for your entire company is a better approach for the following reasons:

- NetWare 4 was designed for enterprise networking, using NDS to create and manage a single network that can be used globally. The whole idea of an enterprise network is for all users and resources to be available on the same network. This gives you a single, seamless method of connecting workstations, servers, and network services throughput the world.

- You cannot share Directory information between Directory trees. Information in one Directory database cannot be seen from any other Directory tree.

- NetWare 4 allows you to "hide" sensitive parts of the tree for security reasons. For example, you could hide the payroll and human resources servers and information from anyone who you determine doesn't need access to those areas. It is easier to set up network security to restrict certain areas than to create and maintain separate Directory trees to limit access.

- As of this writing, the tools necessary to merge separate trees are not available. Novell has indicated that numerous Directory manipulation tools are currently under development and should be included in future releases of NetWare 4.

Planning the top levels of a Directory tree

The very first, or top, level of the Directory tree is the most important, because all other levels of the tree branch from it. Since the top level of the tree is the same for your entire network, its design should be useful and make sense for the entire network.

Whenever possible, design the tree from the top level down. Once you've decided on the top level, proceed down to the next level, then the next, and so on. Be sure to allow your network administrators to provide input on any special needs they may have for the portions of the Directory tree for which they will be responsible. Individual network administrators are probably more familiar with the requirements for their particular network environments.

In large, geographically dispersed networks, we recommend you plan only the top levels of your Directory tree, and then assign individual administrators the responsibility for creating and administering their parts of the tree.

Regardless of your network size, if you distribute the administration of the tree, document specific guidelines for each of your network administrators to follow. This is necessary to maintain uniformity and integrity across your entire network.

How many levels?

NDS supports arbitrary tree depths, with no specified limit as to the number of levels you can have. With this much flexibility, you might be tempted to create a deep Directory tree. However, an unnecessarily complex structure can make using and managing the tree more difficult than it needs to be. It is recommended that you use no more than four or five levels for your Directory tree. With thoughtful planning, four levels should be sufficient for any type or size network.

Remember, each additional level you add to your Directory tree increases the length of your users' contexts. Logically, users remember and can navigate through shorter contexts easier than longer, more complex contexts. By limiting your Directory tree to no more than four levels, you ensure that a user's complete name would never be longer than *Username.OU.OU.OU.O*. This is an ideal scheme recommended for any size of Directory tree. It may not work in all circumstances, but you should try to keep your tree's structure as simple as possible.

NOTE

The [Root] of the Directory tree is not a part of an object's context, and, thus, does not add an additional level to the Directory tree.

The only definite rules in NDS are that every Directory tree must contain at least one Organization container, and Organizational Units (if any) must be one level below the Organization level.

Directory trees can be kept simple by using only one Organization object and as few Organizational Unit objects as you absolutely need to contain all of your Directory objects (network resources and users).

Figure 7-1 shows an example of a simple tree consisting of two levels. This example has Organization as the top level with two subordinate Organizational Units branching from it. Note that the two OUs contain all of the leaf objects in the Directory database.

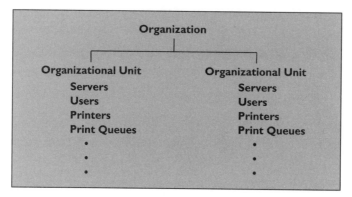

Figure 7-1. A simple Directory tree with two levels.

Simple trees such as this one can be expanded easily as your network grows. You can easily add more Organization and Organizational Unit objects to your Directory tree, and it is easy to install new servers and resources as needed. By implementing your Directory tree in this simple manner, you won't have to redesign your Directory tree every time you need to add additional servers or Organizational Units.

Directory design alternatives

There are many ways to view the logical structure of an organization: organizational chart, physical location, and job functions are three examples.

Organizational chart method

One way to set up your Directory tree is to follow the organization chart for your company. For example, you can designate your company as the Organization (O) object, and then designate the departments or groups in the company as Organizational Unit (OU) objects.

For more advanced networks, you can use multiple Organization objects—one for each of your company's business sites. You might also want to use Organization objects to designate each of the parts of your company that are separate business units or subsidiaries. For example, you could designate different divisions of your company Organization (O) objects, and then designate workgroups or departments (whatever logical groupings your company uses) in your divisions as individual Organizational Unit (OU) objects.

It is important to remember that NDS container objects must form the top levels of the Directory tree. NDS container objects are designed to allow you to efficiently organize and manage your network through relationships of groups of objects (both container and leaf objects).

NDS does not limit the number of peer Organization objects you can create or use. Thus you can add Organization container objects as needed, with each Organization object containing as many Organizational Units as you need.

Following your company's organizational chart can work well for most networks, from the simplest to the most complex. Many administrators prefer this method because it is likely that most people are at least somewhat familiar with the organization of their company. Those users who are familiar with the company's organization will be more likely to remember their user context. By using the standard organization, users also have a map they can follow to move around the Directory tree easily.

Figure 7-2 shows an example of a Directory tree based on a company's organization chart.

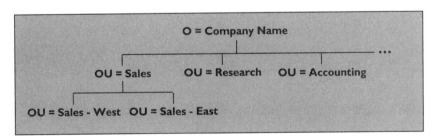

Figure 7-2. A Directory tree based on a company's organizational chart.

Geographic method

Another method for structuring your Directory is to designate geographic locations as Organizational Units. Using a geographic Directory structure can be advantageous because it allows your network users to actually "see" where Directory objects are physically located. This geographical structure is usually most effective for more complex networks. It is rarely advantageous for use on small, simple networks.

If your network users and resources remain static in a geographic Directory structure, this configuration can provide a stable NetWare 4 environment. Be aware that if you have users or network resources that are frequently moved between locations, their contexts can change dramatically even though the organization does not. While this is often a necessity for complex Directory trees and might work well for your network environment, plan carefully before using this Directory design method.

Figure 7-3 shows an example of a geographic Directory tree structure.

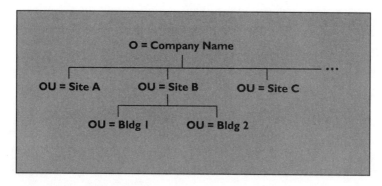

Figure 7-3. A Directory tree using geographic structure as Organizational Units.

Job function method

Another way to structure your Directory tree is by job function. If your company has users or groups that perform identical functions, you might consider organizing your Directory tree according to those job functions.

For instance, if your company has different development teams that are responsible for different products or projects, you might want to set up each product or project group as separate Organizational Units, as in Figure 7-4.

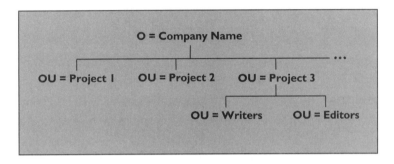

Figure 7-4. A Directory tree using project groups as Organizational Units.

Other design suggestions

As you consider your company's organization, locations, and working environment, you will most likely come up with a Directory tree design that is a hybrid of these methods. The above examples are intended to stimulate your thinking. Do not limit yourself by locking exclusively into one of these specific methods.

Here are some other suggestions for tailoring your Directory tree design to fit your needs:

- **NDS does not require all Organizational Units to be of the same type.** You can designate such things as workgroups, departments, and even divisions as Organizational Units. This ability to define different kinds of Organizational Units in a Directory tree allows network administrators to customize the Directory to fit the needs of their particular network environment. It is often beneficial to define groups in the tree according to how they perceive their place in the overall organization.

- **Choose a Directory organization that will not change frequently.** By reducing the need to change your Directory, you also reduce the amount of administrative tasks you must deal with on your Directory tree.

  For example, in an Accounting department, an accountant may be assigned to work on several different accounting projects. The accountant typically spends a few weeks on each project, and then moves on to the next project for a certain amount of time. If these individual accounting projects are set up as separate Organizational Units, the network supervisor might need to move the accountant's User object between Organizational Units every time the accountant is switched to a different project. The constant moving of the accountant's User object can create both confusion for the accountant as well as headaches for the network administrator, because the accountant's context changes as she or he is moved from project to project.

  If you set up your Organizational Unit to include all of the Accounting department, this eliminates the need to change the location of the accountant's User object (and thus the user's context) and simplifies Directory administration as the accountant moves between projects.

Above all, keep simplicity in mind. Minimize the number of levels in your Directory tree and keep it as simple as possible. Also, make the Directory tree as consistent as possible to reduce potential difficulties during administration and troubleshooting.

Figuring out all of the things you must consider to plan and implement an efficient and useful Directory structure most likely requires that you get input from division managers, department heads, workgroup supervisors, and your information systems (or equivalent) department. With the knowledge and input of these people, your Directory tree should be efficient and fit the needs of your users.

Placing Objects in the Tree

The best way to define NDS container objects and their contents is to identify valid workgroups, shared network resources, and the way information is used and exchanged. After defining these NDS objects, decide which objects represent resources used by each group, and place those objects in the same NDS container as the group members using those resources.

NetWare 4 includes various utilities to add, delete, or move leaf objects after Directory tree installation. These utilities allow you the flexibility to change these things if things don't work out right the first time. However, this ability is currently limited to leaf objects only. You still cannot change container objects with the current utility set.

 NOTE Novell has stated that some future release of NetWare will have utilities that let you change container objects. It appears likely that these utilities will also be made available on Novell's NetWire Forum on the CompuServe Information System. For more information on NetWire, see Appendix B.

It is best to plan ahead so it is not necessary to make radical changes to the Directory tree later.

Placing objects in container objects

NDS allows you to create Organization (O) and Organizational Unit (OU) container objects, as well as leaf objects. Remember these simple rules:

- Organization (O) objects can hold Organizational Unit (OU) objects, leaf objects, or both.

- Organizational Unit (OU) objects can hold other (subordinate) Organizational Unit objects and leaf objects.

- Organizational Unit (OU) objects cannot hold Organization (O) objects. Leaf objects can hold neither Organization (O) nor Organizational Unit (OU) objects.

Try to avoid placing more than 1,500 objects in any NDS container. This will make network administration easier, as current NetWare 4 utilities do not efficiently handle more than 1,500 objects at a time.

This restriction on number of objects is not a shortcoming of the NetWare 4 operating system or NDS, but rather a limitation of the current NetWare 4 utilities.

N O T E

To take full advantage of the Directory, remember to designate and use standard naming conventions for NDS objects and their object properties. If you use a consistent set of names for your Directory objects and their properties, your users will be able to browse and search the Directory more precisely and efficiently. For examples of suggested naming standards, refer to Appendix A.

Installing server objects into an existing Directory tree

You actually "create" the Directory tree by installing NetWare 4 servers and indicating where they belong in the tree's structure. NetWare 4

allows you to install a new server into any existing Directory tree by specifying the existing tree name during the server installation process. Once
this is done, you can then do one of the following:

- Create the new Server object and its Volume objects in a
  new context by creating a brand new container object.
  This is the standard process to use when adding a new
  branch to the Directory tree for such things as a new division, department, or workgroup. This is also the method
  for adding a new container to the tree at whatever level.

  or

- Place the new Server object in a context (container object)
  that already exists in the tree. This allows you to add a
  new server to a pre-existing workgroup, department, and
  so on. You can add a server resource without having to
  add a whole new section to the Directory tree.

Default leaf objects for a new server

Whenever you install a new NetWare 4 server, the installation program
automatically creates and places the following leaf objects in the same
Organization or Organizational Unit where you have placed the new server:

- The NetWare Server object

- Volume objects for volume SYS and all other volumes that
  reside on the server

In addition, the following objects are created (by default) on the first
server installed in a new tree (and always under the first Organization
object):

- The User object Admin. This object is granted all rights to
  the tree so you can login as Admin and begin creating
  objects.

- The User object SUPERVISOR (used for bindery emulation purposes only). This object is only recognized by NetWare 2 or 3 utilities. User SUPERVISOR initially has the same password, but not the same rights, as User Admin.

Default leaf objects from an upgraded server

Whenever a NetWare 2 or 3 server is upgraded to NetWare 4, the Server object is automatically placed in a container object. All objects that were in the bindery (as well as the default leaf objects) are automatically placed in the same container object as the Server object.

Figure 7-5 shows how bindery objects and the upgraded server object are placed in a Directory tree in an Organizational Unit object.

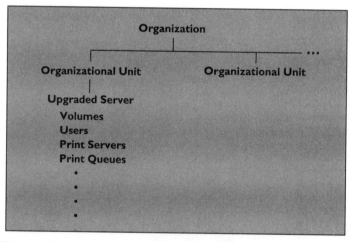

Figure 7-5. A bindery-based NetWare server upgraded to NetWare 4.

Use of various other NDS objects

Chapter 2 introduced the numerous types of objects that are available for use in a NetWare 4 Directory tree. It also gave some examples of what each object type could be used for. Some additional suggestions are given below.

User objects

When planning your Directory tree, carefully consider how and where you place User objects in NDS container objects. The best place to create User objects is in the container object where they will typically login and access network resources.

Avoid creating duplicate User objects for the same person. This can cause network administration problems, as well as problems with Directory rights and contexts. In a pure NetWare 4 environment, it is neither necessary nor advantageous to create duplicate User objects.

If your network will be a mix of NetWare 2 or 3 servers and NetWare 4 servers using bindery emulation, you may have users who need to access servers that reside in different bindery contexts. In this situation, plan carefully to avoid User object duplication, if at all possible. This will save you management headaches in the future, and provides for easier network access by your users. Also keep in mind network security issues when considering having duplicate user objects.

Alias objects

In Chapter 2, we mentioned you can use leaf objects in the management of your Directory tree. An example of this would be the use of the NDS Alias object. The NDS Alias object can be used to represent any shared resource that most network users need access to. For more information on the use of the NDS Alias object, see Chapter 12.

Other objects

Other useful objects you should plan for in your Directory tree include Organizational Role and Directory Map objects. Possible uses for these objects are given in Chapter 2.

Placement of shared resources

While designing your Directory tree, give special attention to any resources that everyone on the network will need access to. For example, if your company has a modem pool or e-mail server to which everyone needs access, you will probably want to place this server in a container that resides above the containers where your User objects are located.

NetWare 4 allows you to grant rights at the container level that allow the users residing in that container to access a particular object. By placing a shared resource in a container that resides above the containers where the User objects reside, you can easily assign rights to the lower containers that allow all of the users in the subordinate containers to access the Server object, as in Figure 7-6.

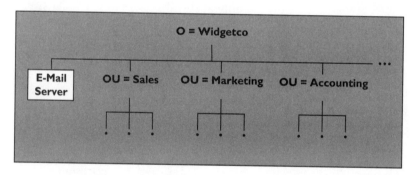

Figure 7-6. Placing a shared resource to grant easy access to everyone.

Evaluating Your Directory Tree Design

A good way to assess the effectiveness of your Directory tree is to map it out on a piece of paper. You can then determine where there is a potential for problems, or see how different parts of the tree might be better placed elsewhere.

It is recommended that you create two maps of the tree. The first and most important is the logical view of the tree. This shows the names and placement of the containers and other objects. The second is a physical view of the placement of replicas. This view shows every server and the replicas stored on each one (see Figure 7-7).

While this is a time-consuming process, drawing out various versions of your Directory tree and discussing the possibilities with those responsible for administration of the various parts of the tree can help you evaluate the best structure for your specific environment.

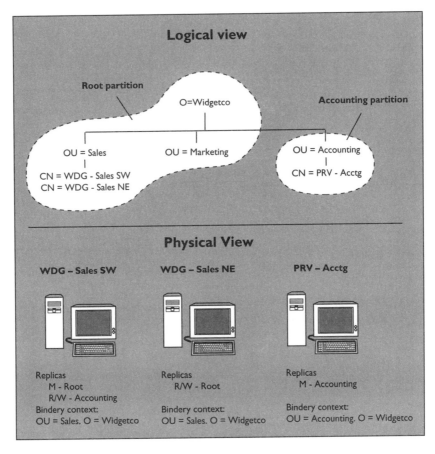

Figure 7-7. Physical and logical views of a Directory tree.

Summary

The information presented in this chapter, and in the six earlier chapters should provide the foundation you need to successfully plan an efficient Directory tree that is easy to use. Because there are so many variables for any network environment, it is hard to provide more than just guidelines for planning a Directory tree. Since there is no one "right way" to design a Directory tree, we have specifically avoided presenting anything that might be construed as hard and fast rules for Directory design.

Use these guidelines to plan and draw out various Directory tree structures you think might work for your specific needs. Don't be afraid to try out these plans on a small pilot network prior to implementation. If you have a small or simple network, you can often use the NetWare 4 installation defaults for your Directory tree.

The main thing to keep in mind when designing your Directory tree is that NetWare 4 gives you flexibility to make your tree fit your network needs, rather than forcing you to design your tree in one set manner. Don't be overwhelmed by the planning process. NDS may be new and different from what you're used to, but if you think things out and use the guidelines in this book, you will be able to plan a Directory tree structure that will make your life as a network administrator easier, your network resources more available for sharing, and your business more productive.

Section 2

Implementing NetWare Directory Services

Migrating Your Servers to NetWare 4

Given Novell's dominant share of the PC networking market, a large number of those who decide to move to NetWare 4 will already have NetWare servers installed. This chapter provides an overview of the steps necessary to successfully upgrade (or migrate) servers from previous versions of NetWare. It also talks about the different methods and utilities that are available to help you migrate existing data and resources into a new NetWare 4 network.

Novell provides two utilities for migrating to NetWare 4 from previous versions of NetWare: the In-Place Migration Utility and the Across-the-Wire Migration Utility. While it is beyond the scope of this book, you can also use these utilities to upgrade to NetWare 4 from other vendors' network operating systems, such as Microsoft's LAN Manager and IBM's LAN Server.

If you are planning a migration from NetWare 3.1 or later, you can perform the migration using the NetWare 4 INSTALL program, without using the migration utilities. No matter which version of NetWare you currently use, your migration will proceed more smoothly if you read and follow the helpful hints given in the first part of this chapter.

The NetWare 4 Migration Process

Novell uses the term *migrate* rather than upgrade because much of the existing NetWare-specific data actually is converted into a new format (from bindery to NDS). The process of migrating to NetWare 4 includes the following phases:

- Installing new client software on DOS/Windows workstations.

- Converting bindery objects from the previous NetWare version to the corresponding NDS objects in NetWare 4.

- Upgrading previous NetWare volumes to NetWare 4 volumes, while keeping the contents completely intact.

- Installing new NLMs, drivers, utilities, and other server software.

N O T E   NetWare 4 includes a new feature known as *data migration,* which allows you to free up server disk space by moving unused data to a mass storage device such as optical disk or tape. This type of migration is completely different from the server migration discussed in this chapter.

Installing the new DOS client software

In the past, the first task in upgrading to a new version of NetWare was usually to install the new operating system on the file servers. However, to take advantage of all of NetWare 4's new features as quickly as possible, it is recommended that you upgrade your workstation (client) software first.

NetWare 4 requires new client software for DOS/Windows users to take advantage of its enhanced features. This new client software, known as the NetWare DOS Requester or Virtual Loadable Modules (VLMs), provides the same functionality as the NETX shell. It can also be used with previous versions of NetWare in place of NETX. Thus if you upgrade the clients first, they can still access the existing, unmodified servers, but will have instant access to the NetWare 4 features as soon as your servers are migrated. All you need to do is make a few quick modifications to the users' NET.CFG files.

Chapter 10 provides more information on the VLM client software and the NET.CFG modifications you need to make.

Preparing NetWare 2 or 3 servers for migration

Once you have planned your Directory tree structure, it is wise to devise a plan for migrating your existing NetWare file servers to NetWare 4. Adequate preparation simplifies the migration process and helps your network turn out the way you planned it. This section outlines some preparatory steps to take before migrating your servers.

Cleaning up the bindery

The biggest part of your preparation deals with cleaning up the existing bindery on the server to be migrated. Cleaning up the bindery means preparing the bindery so the bindery objects transfer cleanly to the new Directory database as valid NDS objects. By doing this, you avoid many possible problems that might result from simply bringing the bindery objects across to NDS without any preparation.

1. Make sure all bindery object names conform to the NDS naming standards established in your NDS Naming Standards Document (see Appendix A for a sample document). Modifying the object names now not only makes the migration easier, it also gives your users a chance to become familiar with the new NDS object names and naming standards. This simplifies their use of the Directory tree.

2. Delete any bindery objects that are no longer being used, such as user accounts for people who no longer need access to your server or who have left the company. For help in determining which bindery objects are no longer valid or necessary, Novell's Systems Research Department has developed two handy utilities called PRINTUSR and PRINTGRP. These utilities print a list of all defined users and groups for a particular server. The programs are available on CompuServe in Novell's NetWire forum, in a file called AN304X.ZIP in NOVLIB 11 (type **go novlib**). Since these utilities are provided free, they are not supported by Novell Technical Support.

3. Make sure you don't have any bindery objects that are of different types, yet have the same name. For instance, it is possible to have both a user and a print queue named MAC. Novell's Systems Research Department also has a DUPBIND utility that scans the bindery and reports any duplicate object names. This utility is included in the AN304X.ZIP file. Even though these utilities are not supported software, they are useful in preparing your network for migration.

4. When you have completed the three previous steps, do a complete backup of the server's file system. Then run the NetWare BINDFIX utility. If BINDFIX fixes any problems that existed in your bindery, make another complete backup of the file system.

User accounts on multiple servers

Now is a good time to check for users who have accounts on multiple servers. If the NetWare 4 INSTALL program finds duplicate user names on servers being installed into the same NDS partition, the program lists all users with the same name and asks if you want to:

- Change the username on the second and all successive servers.

  or

- Merge user objects that have the same name into one NDS object.

If you choose the latter option, be aware that user properties (such as password and account restrictions) on the first server migrated take precedence over any like properties on subsequent servers.

If the servers are installed into different NDS partitions, two separate user objects with the same name will exist in the different partitions. The user will be able to log in at either NDS context, but will be able to see different portions of the Directory tree from each context.

T I P

Try to avoid having the same user object located in different NDS contexts. An easier alternative is to come in after installation and delete the user in all but one of the contexts. Then replace the user object in those contexts with an Alias object that points to the user object in the first context.

Another important consideration is user login scripts. If a user has login scripts on two separate NetWare 3 servers, only the user's login script that resides on the first server migrated into a context is carried over into the Directory. If the servers are being migrated into completely different Directory contexts, this won't be a problem.

Cleaning up the file system

Before migrating to NetWare 4, you should also clean up the file system on the NetWare server you are going to upgrade. You'll need about 70 MB of disk space to hold the complete NetWare 4 operating system, utilities, and online documentation. Also, the NetWare In-Place Migration utility requires about 50 MB of free disk space on the SYS volume for the

INSTALL program to use for temporary file storage during the migration process. While smaller binderies require less space, we recommend you have no less than 50 MB free.

In the process of freeing disk space for the migration, you might want to remove directories that aren't being used, such as those containing obsolete applications or home directories of users no longer on the server.

Always back up your server's file system after cleaning up the file system, but immediately prior to migrating your server.

Check the NetWare 4 hardware requirements

Some of your existing servers may need a hardware upgrade before they can be used for NetWare 4. NetWare 4 requires a 386 or 486 PC with at least 8 MB of RAM and about 70 MB of disk space for the operating system. You may need even more RAM if you are loading numerous NLMs and additional name space support (such as for Macintosh and OS/2 clients).

If you need a more precise RAM estimate or guidelines for other hardware requirements, refer to the *NetWare 4 Installation and Upgrade* manual or to the April 1993 Special Edition of the *NetWare Application Notes* available from Novell Systems Research. If you have not yet purchased NetWare 4 and need information on hardware requirements, you can call 1-800-NETWARE and request information on NetWare 4's hardware requirements.

Drivers, NLMs, and other server software

Most of the necessary LAN and disk drivers you'll need come with the NetWare 4 software. You should use these driver versions (or newer NetWare 4 certified drivers if available).

When upgrading LAN drivers, you should be aware that Novell has changed the default Ethernet frame type for all drivers shipped with NetWare 4 from ETHERNET_802.3 to ETHERNET_802.2. The NetWare

4 INSTALL program (by default) enables server support for *both* the 802.3 raw and IEEE 802.2 frame types. This ensures that any routers or client workstations using the 802.3 frame type can still access the server. However, we recommend you phase out 802.3 and use the 802.2 frame type exclusively whenever possible. This decreases overall network traffic and prepares your network for emerging technologies that rely on 802.2 frames. (Note that all NetWare Token Ring drivers already support the IEEE 802.2 functionality.)

While many NetWare 3.1x NLMs work under NetWare 4, some do not, especially those that rely heavily on the bindery. Check with your Novell reseller or the NLM vendor to determine NetWare 4 compatibility. You may need to keep a few NetWare 3 servers around until more NetWare 4 certified NLMs become available.

Developing a Coexistence Strategy

In most cases, you won't be upgrading all of your servers and clients to NetWare 4 overnight—it will probably take some time to make the transition. You will need a plan to deal with the period during which you have both NetWare 4 servers and previous versions running on the same network.

The main thing to plan for is the use of bindery emulation. As described in Chapter 6, this feature allows non-NDS clients and programs to log in to NetWare 4 servers. Although they won't be able to use Directory Services features, non-NDS clients can run applications and access data on NetWare 4 servers. If you haven't already done so, read Chapter 6 and follow its guidelines for using bindery emulation on your network.

N O T E Bindery emulation is necessary to support Macintosh clients, even if you install the version of NetWare for Macintosh that comes with NetWare 4.01. Native NDS support for Macintosh and other non-DOS clients will be provided in future releases.

Another consideration to plan for is the addition of Server and Volume objects for NetWare 2 or 3 servers into your NetWare 4 Directory tree. You can use the NETADMIN or NWAdmin utilities to create these objects for a non-NetWare 4 server. That way, NDS clients can see the servers when they browse the Directory and access data on the volumes the same as NetWare 4 volumes.

While you can create Server and Volume objects, *do not* use NETADMIN or NWAdmin to create User, Printer, or other objects for a NetWare 2 or 3 server. You may end up losing the passwords, login scripts, and trustee rights assignments stored in the bindery for these objects. Instead, use the NetWare migration utilities and the NetWare 4 INSTALL program to migrate bindery objects to NDS.

Migration Methods

Novell provides three methods for migrating from NetWare 2 or 3 to NetWare 4. The available methods are:

1. In-Place Migration.

2. Across-the-Wire Migration to the same server (same server option).

3. Across-the-Wire Migration to a new NetWare 4 server (new server option).

Each of these methods has specific advantages and disadvantages, as listed in Figure 8-1. Carefully consider the pros and cons of each method before deciding which one is best for your situation.

The following sections provide an overview of each migration method. For more detailed information, refer to the NetWare 4 documentation or to the documentation that comes with the NetWare migration utilities.

Method	Advantages	Disadvantages
In-Place	No additional hardware is required.	Can't be accomplished from NetWare 2.0a or 3.0.
Across-the-Wire to the same server	You can choose what data you migrate. You can specify where you want the data to go (specific volume or file system directory) so you can keep old system files seperate from the NetWare 4 system files.	Requires a workstation with enough hard disk space to hold data during the migration process. There is a risk of data loss, as the data on the original server is overwritten when NetWare 4 is installed.
Across-the-Wire to an installed NetWare 4 server	You can migrate more than one server to a single server. You can specify which data to migrate. You can specify where you want the data to go (specific volume or file system directory) so you can keep old systems files seperate from the NetWare 4 system files. There is no risk of data loss as the original server still exists intact.	You need additional hardware in the form of an existing NetWare 4 server.

Figure 8-1. Advantages and disadvantages of the three migration methods.

The In-Place Migration method

Novell developed the In-Place Migration utility to facilitate the migrata-tion of a NetWare 2.x server to NetWare 3.1x. This intermediate step is necessary when migrating from NetWare 2.x to NetWare 4. If you are migrating from NetWare 3.1x to NetWare 4, the NetWare 4 INSTALL program handles the migration. The INSTALL program's main menu includes an option for upgrading from NetWare 3.1x to NetWare 4.

The In-Place Migration method is best if you are currently running NetWare 2.1x (any version above 2.0a) or 3.1x (any version above 3.0), and you want to upgrade the server without using another server or client workstation to complete the upgrade.

The In-Place Migration software includes an NLM called 2XUPGRDE.NLM and a special version of the NetWare 3.11 SERVER.EXE program. After loading this SERVER.EXE on a NetWare 2.1x server, you run the NLM to transform the existing NetWare partition into a NetWare 3.1x partition. No data is lost during this process. Once the partition is NetWare 3 compatible, you use the NetWare 4 installation program to complete the migration process.

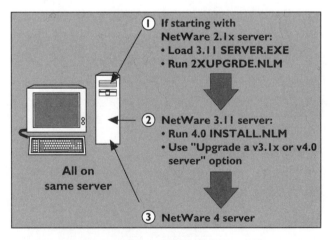

Figure 8-2. The In-Place Migration method.

The 2XUPGRDE.NLM ships with all versions of NetWare 4 after version 4.0. However, the utility has been enhanced since the initial release of NetWare 4. For best results, you should use version 1.10 or higher. You can download the latest version from the NOVLIB area of NetWire on CompuServe. The file to download is called 2XTO3X.EXE. This self-extracting compressed file includes the following files:

- 2XUPGRDE.NLM (the In-Place Upgrade NLM)

- 2XUPGRDE.DOC (documentation for the In-Place Upgrade in ASCII format)

- ERRORS.DOC (system messages for the In-Place Upgrade in ASCII format)

- README.UPG (file documenting the latest changes to the In-Place Upgrade NLM)

Since the necessary documentation for this utility is provided with the software, we won't go into the specifics of running this utility in this book.

Across-the-Wire Migration to the same server

The Across-the-Wire Migration utility (AMU) facilitates the migratation of a NetWare 2 or 3 server to NetWare 4. This utility has a same server option that lets you migrate to NetWare 4 on the same server. To do this, you must have a DOS client workstation that has enough available hard disk space to store your server's data temporarily. Alternatively, you can use a workstation that has an adequate tape drive.

The first step in this method is to back up the existing server's data to the workstation. You then use the AMU (MIGRATE.EXE program) to convert its bindery information to NDS information. All of this information is stored on the workstation. Once that is done, you run the NetWare 4 installation program on the server to install the new operating system and NDS. Once NetWare 4 is installed on the server, you need to upgrade the workstation to the new NetWare 4 client (VLM) software. You then use the AMU to migrate the converted bindery information into the NDS database. Finally, you restore the data stored on the workstation to the NetWare 4 server. The AMU converts the server and bindery information automatically. Figure 8-3 illustrates this process.

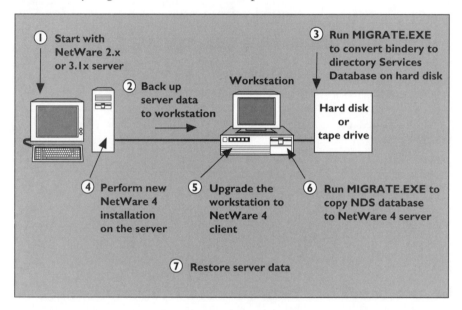

Figure 8-3. Across-the-Wire Migration to the same server.

As with the NetWare In-Place Upgrade utility, the Across-the-Wire Migration Utility (MIGRATE.EXE) comes with NetWare 4. However, the most current version is available in the NOVLIB section of NetWire on CompuServe. This utility includes the necessary files to use the AMU utility for both the same server and new server options.

Remember, to use this method, you must have a DOS workstation with enough free hard disk space to hold all of the necessary server data and bindery files. There is also a potential for data loss, as the original data is overwritten when NetWare 4 is installed on the server.

Across-the-Wire to a new NetWare 4 server

The Across-the-Wire Migration utility also has a new server option to let you migrate server data and bindery information to a new NetWare 4 server. Once you install NetWare 4 on the new server machine, you run MIGRATE.EXE on a DOS client workstation to convert the old server's bindery into NDS information on the new server. You then copy file system data directly from the old server to the new server. This migration process is illustrated in Figure 8-4.

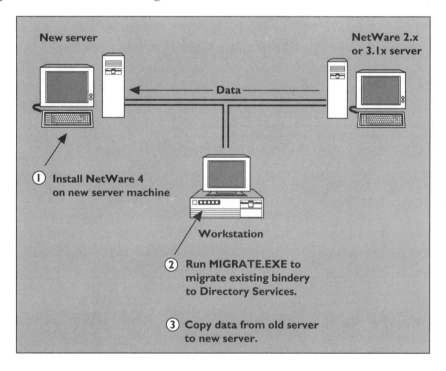

Figure 8-4. Across-the-Wire Migration to a new server.

This method provides more flexibility because you can take information currently residing on a 286 server and migrate it to a 386 or 486 machine to run NetWare 4. It also allows you the opportunity to merge or consolidate information from several servers on one NetWare 4 server. To reduce administration and software/hardware costs, you might want to consider consolidating a number of NetWare 2 and 3 servers into one NetWare 4 server. NetWare 4 is currently available in versions that can handle up to 1,000 users concurrently.

You also have the option of selecting exactly what data to migrate, as well as to which volumes or file system directories the data is migrated. This allows you to keep existing system files separate from the NetWare 4 system files.

When migrating to a new server, you eliminate the potential risk for data loss that exists with the AMU same server option. Since your current server remains intact throughout the migration process, your data is safe. The one disadvantage to using the AMU's new server option is the cost of new server hardware for your NetWare 4 server. Note that it also requires a DOS client workstation. If this method best suits your needs, it is preferable to running the AMU utility with the same server option.

Summary

This chapter covered the steps you need to complete prior to migrating servers from NetWare versions 2 and 3 to NetWare 4. If you follow these steps carefully and use the utilities described in this chapter, your network migration should proceed smoothly.

Setting Up NDS During NetWare 4 Installation

O nce you've planned out all aspects of your Directory tree structure and established any necessary NetWare 4 migration and coexistence strategies, you are ready to begin the actual NetWare 4 installation process. All of your careful planning will finally pay off as you install or upgrade your servers one by one to implement the Directory tree you have designed.

This chapter does not cover the entire NetWare 4 server installation process. It focuses mainly on those parts of the process that are directly related to NDS. It discusses the critical steps that involve NDS and explain how to implement these items. It also covers the NDS defaults and available options. For instructions on the whole installation process and the parameters required to take advantage of all NetWare 4 features, refer to the NetWare 4 documentation.

The procedure for NDS installation is slightly different for the first server than for subsequent ones. Accordingly, this chapter takes you through the NDS installation process for the first server in a new Directory tree. After that, it takes you through the steps necessary to install a NetWare 4 server into an existing Directory tree.

Follow Your Plan

Before starting a NetWare 4 installation, you should have already formulated your Directory Services plan. The plan should be detailed enough so you know where each server will be located in the Directory tree, how the tree will be partitioned, which servers will hold Master replicas and which will have Read/Write or Read/Only replicas, and what type of time server each server will be. You should also have hardware configuration information close at hand for the server CPU, network adapters, disk drives, optical drives, and so on.

To help you compile this information in a usable form, some sample installation worksheets are included in Appendix C. Copy these worksheets and fill them out for each NetWare 4 server you will install. It is also helpful to have a diagram of your network's Directory structure.

Installation Process for the First NetWare 4 Server

The NetWare 4 installation process involves many steps. Again, this book focuses on those steps that deal directly with setting up NDS. Use this information as a reference to supplement the NetWare 4 installation documentation.

Here are a few general installation tips that may be of help:

- Although you can install NetWare 4 from floppy diskettes, the preferred way is to install from a CD-ROM drive. The NetWare 4 software comes on a CD, so it is well worth the investment to purchase a CD-ROM drive if you don't already have one. You must order floppy diskettes separately from Novell if you want to use them instead.

- The NetWare 4 INSTALL program generates random network addresses for you during installation. INSTALL searches your network and verifies that these addresses are unique, so there is no danger of duplication. However, larger networks are easier to manage if there is a system in place for assigning addresses for both cable segments and internal IPX net numbers. Each new cable segment could be assigned an address before it is installed. Divisions in your organization could be assigned ranges of addresses that only they can use.

- If you are migrating to NetWare 4, it is a good idea to install the new VLM client software on your DOS workstations first. The VLMs work with NetWare 4 and with previous versions of NetWare. Users can continue to access NetWare 2 or 3 servers, and then switch over to NetWare 4 servers as soon as they are installed.

  Even if you are performing a new NetWare 4 installation, set up at least one DOS/Windows client so you can run the NetWare administration utilities to fine tune your Directory tree implementation.

- Instead of installing NetWare 4 servers as you may have done in previous versions of NetWare, consider designating certain servers for specific functions. For instance, you could have one server as an application server on which you load word processing, spreadsheet, and other applications. Another server could be a dedicated database server, yet another an e-mail server, and so on. You could even have a login server specifically for users' home directories and login information.

- The computer you install as the root server (the first server you create) should be the most optimized machine you have. At least a 486/25MHz PC with plenty of RAM and fast LAN and disk channels is recommended. This server needs to be fast because it holds your root container object and usually the Master replica of your root partition. A lot of traffic passes through this server; it needs to be fast so overall network performance won't be degraded.

- Do not load any type of memory-management program (including the EMM386 that comes with most recent versions of DOS) on the server PC. The SERVER.EXE program will not load if a memory manager is present.

First step: setting the server time

Before you begin installing NetWare 4, you need to complete a simple but important step: You must run the SETUP program or use the SET TIME command on the computer that is going to be used as your NetWare 4 server and correctly set the server's time as close to the exact local time as possible.

WARNING

While this may seem to be trivial matter, it is quite important. As discussed in Chapter 5, Directory Services relies on proper network time and time synchronization to ensure accurate updates to the Directory's database. If you do not set the server's time to the accurate local time prior to installation of NetWare 4, you may encounter problems. This simple step ensures assures accurate time for the network and NDS.

Running the NetWare 4 INSTALL program

Begin the NetWare 4 installation process according to the instructions provided in the Netware 4 documentation. The full documentation is found on the NetWare 4 CD-ROM. You should read the *Installation and Upgrade* manual prior to installation. This chapter assumes you have already read this documentation and are familiar with how to move through the process up to the point of installing NetWare Directory Services.

After you boot the computer, run SERVER.EXE, name the new server, and load INSTALL.NLM to start the NetWare 4 installation process. You will load necessary disk and LAN drivers and then copy the operating system files before you reach the Directory Services portion of the program.

NOTE On-line help is available throughout the entire installation program. The bottom of the screen contains information relevant to the current screen, and tells you how to access the help screens. If you need help filling in a specific field, press the **F1** key for context-sensitive help information.

Specifying the Directory tree name

At this point in the installation process, the INSTALL program examines the network looking for any existing Directory trees. For the *first* NetWare 4 server installed, the INSTALL program announces it could not find a Directory tree. A question box is displayed asking if this is the first Directory server being installed. Answer **Yes.**

Since you are creating a new Directory tree, a prompt asks you to name the Directory tree. Enter a name for your Directory tree.

Filling in time-synchronization information

When installing a NetWare 4 server, you need to specify the time zone in which the server resides. You will be presented with a list of predefined time zones from which to choose. Move the cursor to the proper time zone and press **Enter.**

NOTE If your time zone is not listed in the time synchronization screen, press **Insert** and enter the appropriate information into the fields on the Verify/Enter Time Configuration Information for This Server screen.

Next, you will see the **Verify/Enter Time Configuration Information For This Server** screen, as shown in Figure 9-1.

```
┌────────────────────────────────────────────────────────────┐
│        View/Enter Time Configuration Information for This Server │
├────────────────────────────────────────────────────────────┤
│ Time server type:                 Single Reference          │
│                                                             │
│ Standard time zone abbreviation:                            │
│ Standard time offset from UTC:                              │
│                                                             │
│ Does your area have daylight savings time (DST):            │
│ DST time zone abbreviation:                                 │
│ DST offset from standard time:                              │
│ DST Start:                                                  │
│ DST End:                                                    │
└────────────────────────────────────────────────────────────┘
```

Figure 9-1. The time synchronization configuration information screen.

It is important that you accurately fill in all of the applicable fields. You should have already planned time synchronization for your network and have the necessary information written down and close at hand. This saves you time and minimizes the number of questions for which you might have to track down answers.

The first three fields are for entering the type of time server you are installing, the standard time zone abbreviation for the time-zone in which your server resides, and how much local time differs from UTC (Universal Time Coordinated time, or what was previously known as Greenwich Mean Time). Neither the second nor third field has usable defaults. You must enter the correct information to provide accurate time synchronization.

1. For the first server in a tree, the default *Time server type* is Single Reference. If you are using the default time synchronization configuration, leave this as it is. If you are customizing your configuration with Reference and Primary Time Servers, change the time server type in this field according to your plan.

2. In the *Standard time zone abbreviation* field, enter a three-letter abbreviation for the time zone your in which server resides. For instance, in Utah the correct abbreviation for this field would be MST for Mountain Standard Time. If you do not live in an area that uses a standard time-zone abbreviation, you may enter your own three-letter abbreviation in this field.

3. In the *Standard time offset from UTC* field, enter the local time offset from UTC. This step is extremely important to get right, so read the on-line help carefully. If you aren't sure how many hours' difference there is between your local time zone and UTC time, refer to the chart of world time zones in the NetWare 4 documentation. After entering the correct offset in hours, press **Enter** to toggle to Ahead if your server's time zone is east of UTC, or toggle to Behind if your server's time zone is west of UTC. For example, in Utah the offset would be 7:00:00 BEHIND because Mountain Standard Time is seven hours behind UTC time.

The next five fields contain information about Daylight Savings Time (DST). Again, these fields must be filled in accurately for proper time synchronization.

1. *Does your area have daylight savings time (DST)?* The first field requires a Yes or No answer.

   If the answer is No, you don't need to fill in the remaining fields. Press the **F10** key followed by the **Enter** key to save your time configuration information and exit the time synchronization phase of the NDS installation.

   If the answer in the first DST field is yes, you must fill in all of the other fields accurately. If you do not do this, you

157

will experience time synchronization problems when other servers on the network are changed to daylight savings time and this one is not.

2. The *DST time zone abbreviation* is a three-letter abbreviation similar to the standard time-zone abbreviation entered earlier. In Utah, the abbreviation would be MDT for Mountain Daylight Time. Again, if you do not have a standard abbreviation, you can make one up. You must enter something in this field, because internal NetWare algorithms assume that if no DST abbreviation string is specified, the local custom is not to observe Daylight Savings Time.

3. In the *DST offset from standard time* field, enter how much clocks should be changed when you switch from standard time to Daylight Savings Time in your time zone. The default here is 1:00:00 AHEAD. If daylight savings time in the time zone of your server varies more or less than the one hour default time, you can adjust the time offset to whatever you need. The offset is read in hours, minutes, and seconds, in that order, with each of the three separated by a colon.

4. The *DST Start* and *DST End* fields require you to enter information about when Daylight Savings Time starts and ends. These can be either specific dates and times (such as April 3, 2:00 am and October 30, 2:00 am) or rules that will work no matter what year it is. The possible formats for DST Start are:

```
APRIL 3 2:00 AM
APRIL SUNDAY FIRST 2:00 AM
APRIL SUNDAY >= 1 2:00 AM
```

Similarly, the possible formats for DST End are:

```
OCTOBER 30 2:00 AM
OCTOBER SUNDAY LAST 2:00 AM
OCTOBER SUNDAY <= 31 2:00 AM
```

By using rules instead of specific dates, you eliminate the need to reset the DST Start time every year by "telling" the operating system to use the first Sunday in April and the last Sunday in October as the change dates. You can use whatever format works best for you. Follow the on-screen prompts to decide which format to use. Use the same format for both fields.

Note that you can also set these parameters using the SET server command. Refer to the NetWare 4 documentation for details.

Once all of the DST fields are set properly, save and exit the time configuration process by pressing **F10** followed by the **Enter** key.

Setting the server context

The **Specify A Context For This Server and Its Objects** screen displays next. The server context specifies where in the Directory tree a particular server is located. The screen has information fields for the Organization level and up to three levels of Organizational Units, as shown in Figure 9-2.

This information determines exactly where the NDS Server object will be created for this server in the Directory tree. Again, if you have your Directory tree structure documented, you will be able to easily fill in these fields accurately.

```
┌─────────────────────────────────────────────────────────────┐
│              Directory Services Server Context                │
├─────────────────────────────────────────────────────────────┤
│ Company or Organization:                                      │
│ Level 1 Sub-Organizational Unit (optional):                   │
│ Level 2 Sub-Organizational Unit (optional):                   │
│ Level 3 Sub-Organizational Unit (optional):                   │
│                                                               │
│ Server Context:                                               │
│                                                               │
│ Administrator Name:                                           │
│ Password:                                                     │
└─────────────────────────────────────────────────────────────┘
```

Figure 9-2. The server context information screen.

- The *Company or Organization* field requires the name of the Organization container you are using *at the top* of your Directory tree. The INSTALL program assumes, possibly incorrectly, that you want to use your company name for the Organization container.

- The fields for OU Levels 1, 2, and 3 are optional, but you need to use them to further specify your server's context. You are not limited to the three levels indicated on the screen—you can actually enter up to 25 levels of Organizational Units. The only stipulation is that you must use a period (.) as a delimiter between each name entry.

Since the first server is usually placed at the top of the tree, you will normally enter just the Organization name when installing the first server.

The information in the Server Context field is updated every time a new container name is entered. Once all of the necessary context information is entered, press the **Enter** key.

- The *Administrator's Name* field contains the Common Name (CN) of the administrator for this part of the Directory tree. The default is CN=ADMIN, for which a User object is created automatically by the installation process. You can change this name to something else. If you do, be sure to document the name, the context, and the tree name so you can refer to this information later. At this point in the installation, it is better to stick with ADMIN. If necessary, you can change the name after the installation process is complete by using the NETADMIN utility.

- In the *Password* field, enter a password for this administrator. This is an optional field, but for security reasons I *strongly* recommend you enter a password. This password will be used from now on to authenticate the administrator to the Directory. Once you've entered the password, press **Enter** and retype the password for verification. If you are afraid you might forget this password, write it down and keep it in a secure place, such as a locked file cabinet or safe.

When you have finished entering the proper information for all of the fields in this screen, press **F10** to save the information.

You should see a message stating that NDS is being installed. This could take a few moments, so be patient. INSTALL displays a message that indicates how many volumes were installed into the Directory. For your reference, it then displays the Directory tree name, context, and administrator name for the server you just installed. Press **Enter** after reading and recording this information for future reference.

This completes the NDS portion of the NetWare 4 server installation. The next step should be to view the STARTUP.NCF file and make any necessary modifications. We are only discussing the NDS specifics here, so continue on with the installation process as instructed on-screen.

Adding a NetWare 4 Server to an Existing Directory Tree

The procedure for installing subsequent servers into your Directory tree is almost the same as for the first server. As before, you must set the server's time to the exact local time. This step is extremely important, especially for servers that will be time sources.

Once this step is completed, start the NetWare 4 INSTALL program according to instructions provided in the Netware 4 documentation. The discussion below starts at the point in the program where you install Directory Services.

Choosing a Directory tree

At this point in the installation process, the INSTALL program lists all Directory trees visible from the server being installed. The Directory tree created when you installed your first NetWare 4 server is in this list. If there is more than one existing tree, be sure to choose the right one for server installation. The server you are currently installing will become a part of the tree you select.

If there are several trees in your company, but the tree you are looking for doesn't appear in the list (possibly due to router or SAP filtering), you can press **F3** to help the program find any additional trees. Once you press **F3**, you are asked to enter the node address of another server. Enter the IPX internal net number of another NetWare 3 or NetWare 4 server on the internetwork. (For a NetWare 2 server or Novell router, enter the network address and node number.) This server or router may have access to Directory trees that the server you are installing does not.

I recommend you avoid this method unless you have a specific need to use it. In a standard installation, you should be able to see the proper Directory tree from your server. To take full advantage of the NetWare 4 feature set, you should only use one Directory tree. Remember, the main idea behind an enterprise network is that the entire network should be a single, efficient entity.

Filling in time-synchronization information

When adding a server to an existing tree, you need to install the server into the proper time zone. As before, INSTALL presents an on-screen list of predefined time zones from which you can choose.

The next screen is the same as before: Verify/Enter Time Configuration Information For This Server. You need to fill in the following information:

1. The type of time server you are installing (the default in this case would be Secondary).

2. The standard time-zone abbreviation.

3. The local time offset from UTC time.

4. Daylight Savings Time information, if applicable.

If the information in the Time Configuration Information screen is incorrect, carefully go through the fields and enter the proper information. Once you've entered and verified the information in this screen, press **F10** to save it. A message is displayed while the time is being synchronized across the network.

Placing the server in the desired context

This next screen prompts you for the administrator's name for this part of the Directory tree. Enter the complete name of your administrator, including the correct context. For example, for the Admin object in an Organization container named XYZ, you would enter the following:

```
CN=ADMIN.O=XYZ
```

Remember, there can be different administrators in different contexts in the Directory tree. The Admin in each context has specific rights over that specific part of the Directory tree. The default is ADMIN, but you could also have specified a user's login name, or even the name of a User object that has the Supervisor object right to this specific context.

Once you've entered the proper name for your administrator, type the administrator's password. Be sure to use the password for the specific Admin in the current context. You should have different passwords for each Admin that has dominion over each specific part of the Directory tree.

Now that you are authenticated as an administrator, you must place the server you are adding to the Directory tree into the proper context. The server context screen looks the same as before. This time, though, you can view the existing Organization and Organizational Unit containers. Press **Enter** at each field to traverse the tree and choose the proper context for server installation.

You are also given the opportunity to define a new context for server installation. If this is what you choose to do, the context you define is added to the existing tree if it considered to be a valid context.

N O T E

You can also expand your Directory tree after installation by using the NetWare Administration utilities to add container objects.

Once you have chosen the proper context, press **F10** to save the context information. Directory Services are installed on the new server, and you can then continue with the NetWare 4 installation process. If you need more help, refer to the on-line help, the NetWare 4 installation manual, or the April 1993 issue of *NetWare Application Notes* to complete your installation.

Whenever you add a server to the Directory, be sure to go back afterwards and check the NDS partitions. If you are not using the default partitioning scheme, you will have to use the NetWare partition management utilities to distribute the partitions the way you want them. Also check to make sure bindery emulation is properly set up for servers that will be accessed by non-NDS clients. Refer to Chapters 4 and 6 for more information on partitions and bindery emulation.

Example: Setting Up the Widgetco Tree

Now that you have some general information on what is included in the NDS portion of the NetWare 4 installation procedure, let's go step by step through the process of installing the first few NetWare 4 servers into our sample Widgetco tree. The first server is the Marketing server installed at the headquarters in Cody, Wyoming. We'll then show how the AZ-Sales server would be installed at the Phoenix, Arizona office.

Installing the first server

The following steps show you how to complete the NDS installation portion for the first server in our fictitious company. These instructions pick up in the middle of the installation process, at the point where you set up Directory Services.

1. Since this is the first NetWare 4 server installed, the INSTALL program states that it could not find a Directory tree. Answer **Yes** to the prompt that asks if this is the first Directory server being installed. This means you are creating a new Directory tree.

   A field appears asking you to name the Directory tree. In this example, type in the name **widgetco** for the tree name.

2. From the time zone list, choose **United States of America Mountain Time** because that is the correct time zone for Cody, Wyoming.

3. The next screen is the Time Configuration Information screen. By referring to the time synchronization plan you wrote down for the Widgetco network, you can easily fill in these fields. Since this is a small tree, use the default time synchronization configuration.

   • In the Time server type field, leave the default of **Single Reference** in place.

   • The next field is the Standard time zone abbreviation for the time zone in which the server resides in. In our example, our server resides in Cody, Wyoming which is in the Mountain Time Zone. Enter **MST**, which is the accepted abbreviation for Mountain Standard Time.

   • The Standard time offset from UTC field defines how much local time differs from UTC time. Since MST is seven hours behind UTC time, enter **7:00:00** as the proper time offset. Press **Enter** to toggle to BEHIND because this server's time zone is west of the zero meridian.

4. Fill in the Daylight Savings Time (DST) information in the lower part of the screen.

   • In the field that asks if the area has daylight savings time, enter **yes** because the time zone in Cody, Wyoming does have DST.

   • In the DST time zone abbreviation field, enter **MDT** for Mountain Daylight Time.

- In the DST offset from standard time field, enter **1:00:00 AHEAD**. This means that when you switch to DST, you set the clocks one hour ahead of standard time.

- The DST Start and DST End fields need to indicate when daylight savings time begins and ends during the year so the server can automatically adjust its time accordingly. For these circumstances, enter the information as rules so you don't have to reset the fields every year. In the DST Start field, enter:

  ```
  APRIL SUNDAY FIRST 2:00 AM
  ```

  Similarly, for the DST End field, enter:

  ```
  OCTOBER SUNDAY LAST 2:00 AM
  ```

5. Exit the time configuration screen by pressing the **F10** key, followed by the **Enter** key to save the configuration.

6. Next, you will see the server context screen. This information determines the exact NDS context into which the Server object is installed.

   - In the Company or Organization field, we type **Widgetco** and press Enter.

   - In the Level 1 Sub-Organizational Unit field, type **Cody** and press Enter. The reason you type Cody here is because this is the OU into which you install the first server. You do not need to input information into the Level 2 and Level 3 OU fields at this time.

167

- The Server Context field now displays OU=Cody.O=Widgetco to let you know what the full context is.

7. Next, move down to the Administrator Name field, which contains the default name of the Administrator for this part of the tree (CN=Admin.OU=Cody.O=Widgetco). In this case, simply keep this default and press **Enter.**

8. In the Password field, enter a unique password for this administrator. In this case, type in the password **ERAWTEN.**

   After pressing **Enter,** you are prompted to reenter the password. Again, type **ERAWTEN** and press **Enter** to verify the password. For future reference, record the administrator name and password and store them in a secure place.

9. Press **F10** to save your Directory Services information and continue on to the next part of the installation process.

After you complete the installation process and exit INSTALL, you have a Directory tree named WIDGETCO. At this point, the tree contains one Organization (O=Widgetco) and one Organizational Unit (OU=Cody). You have also installed the Marketing server and created an ADMIN User object in that OU.

Installing the second server

You go now to the regional sales office in Phoenix, Arizona, to install the second server in the tree. This will be the AZ-Sales server, and it will be installed in an OU called Sales, which is subordinate to an OU you will call Phoenix.

Again, these instructions pick up in the middle of the installation process, at the point where you set up Directory Services. The discussion assumes that an internetwork connection exists between the server in Cody, Wyoming, and the server you are installing in Phoenix.

1. Because an NDS tree already exists on the internetwork, the INSTALL program produces a list of all Directory trees visible from the server you are installing. Since there is only one Directory tree (as recommended), highlight the tree name WIDGETCO and press **Enter.**

2. From the time-zone list, again select **Mountain Time** since Phoenix is also in that time zone.

3. The Verify/Enter Time Configuration Information for This Server screen is displayed. In this circumstance, the default information is not all correct. Arizona stays on Standard Time year-round and does not switch to Daylight Savings Time.

   • In the *Time server type* field, keep the default of **Secondary** as specified in your time-synchronization plan. This will be the default setting for all subsequent servers installed in this tree.

   • Again, use **MST** for the standard time zone abbreviation, and **7:00:00 BEHIND** for the standard time offset from UTC.

   • This time, answer **no** to the question *Does your area have daylight savings time.* The remaining DST fields go blank.

4. Press **F10** followed by **Enter** to accept and save your time-synchronization information.

5. A prompt is displayed asking for the complete name of the administrator. This refers to the ADMIN object created for the first server, since you haven't yet defined any other containers and administrators. Enter the complete name of the administrator (including context) and the correct pass-

word to authenticate to the Directory and be able to proceed with the installation. Type **CN=ADMIN.OU=Cody.O= Widgetco**, and then press **Enter** to accept this entry and move to the next field.

6. The next field requires you to enter the Administrator's password. Type in the password for this specific ADMIN, which in this case is **ERAWTEN,** and press **Enter.**

7. Now you arrive at the screen where you must specify the context in to which install your server. In this case, you are installing your server into a new context: an OU called Sales that resides under an OU named Phoenix that resides under O=Widgetco. Once the proper context is entered, set up an administrator name and password for the new context.

8. Press **F10** to save the Directory Services information. The next thing you should see is a status message informing you how many volumes were installed into our Directory tree. Then INSTALL recaps the Directory tree name, context, and administrator name.

From this point on, finish the rest of the NetWare 4 installation process as instructed by the on-screen prompts. Then create the remainder of the Directory tree by installing subsequent servers at their proper locations.

Summary

This chapter has discussed the NDS installation specifics you need to know to implement your Directory tree. It has not provided a complete description of the NetWare 4 installation process. It has discussed only those steps that involve NDS and explained how to implement these items. By following your Directory Services plan and using this chapter as a guide, you should be able to successfully install and implement your Directory tree with a minimum of fuss.

Logging into the Network Using NetWare VLMs

NetWare 4 uses a new kind of DOS client software known as the NetWare DOS Requester or Virtual Loadable Modules (VLMs). The NetWare VLMs take the place of the NETX client shell and provide a more robust and flexible interface for all versions of NetWare (NetWare 4, NetWare 3, NetWare 2, and even Personal NetWare). This chapter provides an overview of the VLM client software and explains what the various modules do. It also provides sample configurations for using the VLMs to login to the network. The last part of the chapter discusses the login procedure and introduces some of the client utilities that are helpful when logging in and working with NDS.

The NetWare DOS Requester (VLMs)

Although its official name is the NetWare DOS Requester (NDR), almost everybody refers to the new DOS client software as "the VLMs". This is because the software is made up of individual *Virtual Loadable Modules*. Together, these modules provide most of the functionality found in the previous NetWare NETX shell. The VLMs also add new capabilities not found in the NETX shell, as you will see in this chapter.

The NetWare VLM architecture is designed to be a true requester, not a shell. As a DOS Requester, it can take advantage of the DOS Int 2Fh redirection capabilities and use DOS internal drive tables. This is how the VLMs handle nonlocal (network) requests for DOS. By incorporating these features directly in the DOS Requester, a lot of the redundancy between NetWare and DOS is eliminated. Since these expanded capabilities became available in version 3.1 of both MS-DOS and PC-DOS, you must be running DOS 3.1 or greater to use the NetWare VLMs.

The VLM architecture allows programmers to write their own modules to add further functionality and provide extended resources to the NetWare DOS client. Modules written to Novell's VLM specification can plug into the NetWare VLM manager and take advantage of its memory management capabilities.

Virtual Loadable Modules

The VLM.EXE program is the Virtual Loadable Module manager and is loaded first to manage the other VLM modules and the memory each module uses. VLM.EXE is basically a terminate-and-stay-resident (TSR) program manager. As mentioned above, any TSR written to Novell's VLM specification can use VLM.EXE to manage it.

The VLM.EXE that comes with NetWare 4 contains a default list of which VLMs to load, and in which order, to make the best use of Directory Services. Thus, VLM.EXE loads itself first, and then manages the loading of the other VLM modules in the order listed in Figure 10-1.

NOTE

If another memory manager is present, VLM.EXE uses it for the actual loading of its modules.

VLM Filename	VLM module
CONN.VLM	Connection Table Manager
IPXNCP.VLM	IPX/NCP Transport module
TRAN.VLM	Transport Protocol Multiplexor
SECURITY.VLM	Enhanced Security module
NDS.VLM	NetWare Directory Services module
BIND.VLM	Bindery Services module
NWP.VLM	NetWare Protocol Multiplexor
FIO.VLM	File Input/Output module
GENERAL.VLM	General Functions module
REDIR.VLM	DOS Redirector module
PRINT.VLM	Printer Redirection module
NETX.VLM	NetWare Shell Compatibility module

Figure 10-1. Default load order of Virtual Loadable Modules.

173

Types of VLMs

The NetWare VLMs can be divided into two different types of modules: multiplexor modules and child modules. VLM multiplexor modules coordinate activities with specific VLM child modules.

The VLM multiplexors include the NWP.VLM and TRAN.VLM modules. The NWP.VLM multiplexor module works with the child modules that control access to Directory Services (the NDS.VLM module), bindery services (the BIND.VLM module), and Personal NetWare (the PNW.VLM module). The NWP module ensures that necessary information that needs to go to a specific service is routed directly to that service.

The TRAN.VLM module coordinates the routing between any of the various transport protocols that can be loaded on a NetWare client workstation. In the first two releases of NetWare 4 (versions 4.0 and 4.01), the only protocol supported is IPX through the IPXNCP.VLM module. The TRAN.VLM module currently allows the IPXNCP.VLM module to provide the TRAN.VLM services directly.

NOTE
Upcoming releases of NetWare 4 may include other protocol modules so you can use other transport modules, such as AppleTalk and TCP/IP.

Child modules are always loaded *before* the multiplexor modules. Thus, the first child module loaded becomes the default module. For example, if you load the NDS.VLM module before you load the BIND.VLM module, your default login will be as a Directory Services client, not as a bindery emulation client. Of course, it also depends on what type of services you initially attach to. If you attach to a NetWare 4 server in bindery emulation, you will be in bindery mode regardless of the VLM load order.

Some VLM modules work in direct relation with one another, while other VLM modules span several layers of network services. For example, the Connection Table Manager (CONN.VLM) spans the DOS Redirection Layer, the Service Protocol Layer, and the Transport Protocol Layer. Because of this, certain tables can be loaded low to provide better performance.

What the NetWare VLM modules do

You have probably noticed that there are quite a few NetWare VLM modules, with the possibility of more modules being added later. This section lists the current VLM modules (as of this writing) and gives a brief description of what each module does.

VLM.EXE

Again, this is the first module loaded and is the manager for all other VLM modules. Actually, VLM.EXE consists of three components: the main executable, a transient memory swap block, and a global memory swap block. These make up about 48K of the VLMs loaded in conventional memory. VLM.EXE determines the order in which the VLM modules should be loaded into the transient memory block to handle requests. It also coordinates with an expanded or extended memory manager to know into which part of memory the modules are loaded.

Once VLM.EXE coordinates the memory size for loading the other VLM modules, it then directs all incoming requests and outgoing replies to their proper destination. This is done by swapping the transient portions of the modules in and out of the transient swap block to fulfill a request.

CONN.VLM

CONN.VLM is the client Connection Table Manager. This is a vital piece of the client software that spans all three NetWare service layers (DOS Redirection Layer, Service Protocol Layer, and Transport Protocol Layer). The CONN.VLM module allocates and keeps track of the total number of connections the VLM client can have. Currently, this is between two and

175

50 connections, but defaults to eight to be consistent with the previous NetWare shell's capacity. The CONN.VLM module provides connection table information to other VLM modules as requested. It also has the added ability to supply APIs for connection handle validity checking, as well as for providing needed connection statistics.

In previous versions of NetWare, the NETX shell was limited to eight connections per workstation. NetWare 4 (using the NetWare VLMs) increases the possible number of connections up to 50. However, to provide optimum performance for your workstation, I recommend you keep the connections to the default of eight. This is also a good idea if you are in a mixed NetWare environment and you are using pre-NetWare 4 utilities or third-party applications that need to use the NETX services.

REDIR.VLM

The REDIR.VLM module is the DOS Redirector portion of the VLM architecture. Basically, requests from applications or command line entries go to DOS first. Before DOS handles the request, it runs down a list, or chain, of requesters to see if any of them will claim the request. If the request is for a network service (such as a File Open call for a file on a network drive), the DOS Requester takes over and handles the request. The exact interaction varies according to the type of request, which drive letter the request was made on, and so on.

GENERAL.VLM

GENERAL.VLM is a general information module that contains several functions that are used by various other VLM modules. These include:

- Creating and deleting search drive mappings
- Getting connection information
- Getting server information
- Providing search modes

- Providing long and short machine names

- Getting last print queue information

NETX.VLM

The NETX.VLM module is used with NetWare's bindery services to ensure backward compatibility with previous NetWare utilities (those that come with NetWare 3 and below). The NETX.VLM module is necessary if you are running any applications that take advantage of the specific API functionality of a previous version of the NetWare shell.

You can get by without loading the NETX.VLM if you meet either of the following conditions:

1. You have only NetWare 4 servers on your network and never access any non-NetWare 4 servers.

2. You access applications on NetWare 3 or 2 servers without using the NetWare utilities that come with those versions (you only use NetWare 4 utilities).

By not loading NETX.VLM, you can reduce the amount of memory required for the VLMs. This can also help improve workstation performance by reducing the number of modules in the VLM request/reply chain.

TRAN.VLM

TRAN.VLM is the Transport Protocol Multiplexor. The NetWare VLM client software currently comes with the necessary module for running IPX (IPXNCP.VLM). As enterprise interoperability becomes an increasingly important issue, Novell will release other transport protocol modules.

NOTE You can currently have TCP/IP or NetWare/IP connections with the DOS Requester, even though no transport protocol VLMs are yet available for them. You simply use Novell's LAN Workplace or new NetWare/IP software packages to provide this functionality.

177

IPXNCP.VLM

The IPXNCP.VLM module is a transport module that is classified as a child process module of the TRAN.VLM module. This module is *not* a replacement for the IPXODI.COM or IPX.COM communications drivers. However, the IPXNCP.VLM module does build valid network packets (those with a proper NCP header and so forth), and transfer the packets to the IPX protocol for transmission over the network cable.

NWP.VLM

The NWP.VLM module is the NetWare Protocol Multiplexor module that coordinates requests and passes them to the appropriate network module. The NWP.VLM module accomplishes these tasks by connecting to the available network services, performing logins and logouts, and handling broadcasts through its various child modules.

NDS.VLM

The NDS.VLM module is one of several network service modules available in the VLM client software. The NDS.VLM module is necessary to login to NetWare 4 Directory Services and to NetWare 4 servers in general. The VLMs give you the option of loading the NDS.VLM (for NDS clients), the BIND.VLM (for bindery-based clients), or both. In NetWare 4, the default is to load both and put NDS.VLM before BIND.VLM.

BIND.VLM

The BIND.VLM module is another network service module available with the VLM client software. The BIND.VLM module is necessary to login as a bindery-based client (if you are logging into or attaching to NetWare servers running NetWare 3 or below). The VLM client software allows you to load the BIND.VLM module, the NDS.VLM module, or both (if necessary). In NetWare 4, the default is to load both and put NDS.VLM before BIND.VLM.

FIO.VLM

The FIO.VLM module is the File Input/Output module. This module is used whenever the workstation accesses files from the network. It includes the Packet Burst (PBURST) and Large Internet Packet (LIP) capabilities.

PRINT.VLM

The PRINT.VLM module handles print job redirection for both NDS and bindery services. This module takes advantage of the FIO.VLM module to speed up network printing services.

AUTO.VLM

The AUTO.VLM module tries to automatically reestablish the client's network connection in the event that the client loses its NCP connection with a server. If the server(s) the client had connections to come back on-line, the AUTO.VLM module reconnects the client to the server and then rebuilds the user's environment. This includes the user's connection status, drive mappings, and printer connections. However, your recovery from the connection loss (in terms of recovering any data files you had open) depends on how the specific application you were running recovers from a connection loss and subsequent reestablishment.

In the first release of NetWare 4, the AUTO.VLM module was set up to work only with Directory Services. Currently, this module also works with bindery services in NetWare 3 and below. Refer to the NetWare 4 documentation for details on how to use AUTO.VLM.

RSA.VLM

The RSA.VLM module provides Novell's RSA encryption scheme for client authentication with NDS. The RSA authentication process is one of the safest forms of encryption protection currently available.

This module must be loaded if the AUTO.VLM module is being used with NDS. RSA.VLM and AUTO.VLM allow the client to reconnect to the

179

servers it was accessing and provides background authentication for the session without requiring the user to login to the network again.

SECURITY.VLM

The SECURITY.VLM module resides at the transport layer and takes advantage of NetWare's enhanced security features to provide additional client security where needed. In previous versions of NetWare, this enhanced security is called NCP packet signing. It offers an extra level of protection for NCP sessions by adding a unique message digest, or signature, to each packet. This assists in preventing the forging of NCP requests to the server.

When you use the SECURITY.VLM module to enhance your security, expect some degradation in performance. Users with 486/50 workstations or faster probably won't notice the degradation, but users with slower workstations will. If network security is vital to your business, this degradation is more than made up for by the enhanced security this module provides.

NMR.VLM

The NMR.VLM module is the NetWare Management Responder module for Novell's Windows- and OS/2-based network management products. When this module is loaded, it acts as the workstation agent, collecting and communicating the workstation's configuration information, statistics, and ODI information and statistics. This module also provides necessary diagnostic capabilities.

While this module is designed to load with the NetWare VLM modules, it is not a part of the NetWare VLM client software. It is an example of a VLM-compatible extension module written to take advantage of the VLM.EXE's memory management capabilities to load the module into memory.

Configuring the VLM Client Software

Now that you have an overview of what the NetWare VLM client software is and what each module does, let's discuss how to configure the VLM modules for an NDS client to take full advantage of the various NetWare features.

Because this book deals specifically with NDS, we do not discuss the installation procedure for the VLM client software. We focus instead on the necessary configuration parameters that can be set in the client's NET.CFG file. If you need installation information, refer to the VLM documentation available with the latest version of the VLM client software kit available on NetWire in the NOVFILES section, or see the April 1993 issue of the *NetWare Application Notes*. (Appendix B gives more information on the *NetWare Application Notes* and how to order them.)

The NET.CFG File

During the loading of the NetWare DOS client software, the ODI LAN drivers load and the NET.CFG file is accessed. Among other things, the NET.CFG file contains network board setting information and NetWare DOS Requester (VLM) loading information. The following listing is an example of the default settings the NetWare client software installation program creates for a client using an NE2000 network adapter:

```
Link Driver NE2000
   PORT 300
   INT 3
   MEM D0000
   FRAME Ethernet_802.3

NetWare DOS Requester
   FIRST NETWORK DRIVE = F
```

The entries that apply to the NetWare ODI drivers are indented under the Link Driver heading in the NET.CFG file. As shown in the previous example, the default settings for the NE2000 network board are I/O port address of 300h, Interrupt 3, and Base Memory Address D0000. The frame type in the example is set to 802.3. This would be the case for a client installation performed on a network that was migrated from NetWare 3.11 to NetWare 4. In NetWare 3.11, the default Ethernet frame type was 802.3. If you are installing on a new, pure NetWare 4 network, the default frame type will be Ethernet_802.2.

The NET.CFG file also has a heading for NetWare DOS Requester. The only default entry under this heading (provided by the INSTALL program) is FIRST NETWORK DRIVE = F. NetWare 4 allows you to use the NET.CFG parameters with just the default settings. If you want to use the default settings, it is not necessary to add parameter entries for that specific parameter to the NET.CFG file.

However, any time you want to use a setting other than the default, the desired parameter with the changed setting must be added to the NET.CFG file. To keep things simple, place any VLM client software parameters under the NetWare DOS Requester heading and indent the entries. This groups all of the VLM-related parameters together and avoids the possibility of some parameters not being active.

Generic NET.CFG parameters can be placed anywhere in the NET.CFG file and do not need to be indented. However, the more orderly these parameters are entered in the file, the easier it is to change or modify them later.

The INSTALL.CFG File

The NetWare 4 DOS Client installation program allows network administrators to enter specific configuration entries to be placed in every client workstation's NET.CFG file. To do this, you must edit the INSTALL.CFG file on the Installation disk. This can be done using any standard text editor.

For example, if you wanted every one of your network DOS clients to have the settings CACHE WRITES=ON and SHOW DOTS=ON, you would edit the INSTALL.CFG file (using your text editor) as follows. First find the [NETCFG] heading in the file, and then type the desired commands under the NETWARE DOS REQUESTER heading. When this file is saved, you will be ready to install your client software on the client workstations. Every time you install a new client using this particular Install diskette, the parameters you set in the INSTALL.CFG file appear in that client's NET.CFG files.

Sample NET.CFG configurations for NetWare 4

This section gives several examples of actual NET.CFG files used to access both NetWare Directory Services and NetWare 3 bindery-based servers. By looking at the samples, you should be better able to understand how each of the VLM modules works and what modules you need to load for specific situations. These are actual working files that NetWare users have implemented in various network environments.

Before we look at the files, you should be aware the VLM client software that comes with NetWare 4 defaults to using NetWare Directory Services for its initial server connection. The VLM client software loads the VLM.EXE module into extended memory (by default), and then loads the following VLM modules in the order shown:

```
CONN.VLM
IPXNCP.VLM
TRAN.VLM
SECURITY.VLM
NDS.VLM
BIND.VLM
NWP.VLM
FIO.VLM
GENERAL.VLM
```

```
REDIR.VLM
PRINT.VLM
NETX.VLM
```

Keep in mind that the order in which the VLM modules load is important. In the previous list, the NDS.VLM module is loaded before BIND.VLM. This is the default order for NetWare 4 and means that the VLM.EXE module attempts to attach to a server running Directory Services before attempting to attach to a bindery-based server. If the VLM.EXE module is unsuccessful in finding an NDS server to attach to, it looks for a bindery-based server.

Example I

The first file is a typical NET.CFG file that was created to serve multiple purposes. It provides enough flexibility so the user can use this file to login to NetWare 4 daily, and easily modify it (using a text editor) when he or she needs to login to NetWare 3 servers. Because this NET.CFG file is used in this way, all of the VLM modules are listed, and the ones that are not being loaded are remarked out by placing a semicolon (;) at the beginning of the line.

Here is the NET.CFG as used for logging into NetWare 4 as a Directory Services client:

```
Link Driver NE2000
     INT 3
     PORT 300
     Frame Ethernet_802.2
;    Frame Ethernet_802.3

SHOW DOTS ON
NETWARE DOS REQUESTER
     CACHE BUFFERS = 5
     PB BUFFERS = 8
```

```
            USE DEFAULTS = OFF
            VLM = CONN.VLM
            VLM = IPXNCP.VLM
            VLM = TRAN.VLM
            VLM = SECURITY.VLM
            VLM = NDS.VLM
            VLM = BIND.VLM
            VLM = RSA.VLM
            VLM = NWP.VLM
            VLM = FIO.VLM
            VLM = GENERAL.VLM
            VLM = REDIR.VLM
            VLM = PRINT.VLM
            VLM = NETX.VLM
            VLM = AUTO.VLM
            PREFERRED TREE = widgetco
        ;   PREFERRED SERVER = GAMBO
            VLM STACK SWITCH = ON
            BIND RECONNECT = ON
            AUTO RETRY = 10
            CHECKSUM = 0
            LARGE INTERNET PACKETS = ON
            CONNECTIONS = 16
            NETWORK PRINTERS = 3
            FIRST NETWORK DRIVE = F
            NAME CONTEXT = "o=widgetco"
            MESSAGE LEVEL = 3
            SIGNATURE LEVEL = 0
```

In this first file, note that two Ethernet frame types are listed. The 802.3 frame type is remarked out, making the 802.2 frame type active. The line for 802.3 frames is retained in the file for ease of switching when the file is used to access only servers that are using Ethernet 802.3 frames, to which NetWare 3 and 2 servers default.

Also note that the PREFERRED SERVER line is remarked out. This is also used for accessing a specified NetWare 3 server.

Example 2

This is the same file, only modified to access a NetWare 3 server using the Ethernet 802.3 frame type:

```
Link Driver NE2000
        INT 3
        PORT 300
;       Frame Ethernet_802.2
        Frame Ethernet_802.3
SHOW DOTS ON
NETWARE DOS REQUESTER
        CACHE BUFFERS = 5
        BUFFER SIZE = 1024
        PB BUFFERS = 8
        USE DEFAULTS = OFF
        VLM = CONN.VLM
        VLM = IPXNCP.VLM
        VLM = TRAN.VLM
;       VLM = SECURITY.VLM
;       VLM = NDS.VLM
        VLM = BIND.VLM
;       VLM = RSA.VLM
        VLM = NWP.VLM
        VLM = FIO.VLM
        VLM = GENERAL.VLM
        VLM = REDIR.VLM
        VLM = PRINT.VLM
        VLM = NETX.VLM
```

```
        VLM = AUTO.VLM
    ;   PREFERRED TREE = widgetco
        PREFERRED SERVER = GAMBO
        VLM STACK SWITCH = ON
        BIND RECONNECT = ON
        AUTO RETRY = 10
        CHECKSUM = 0
        LARGE INTERNET PACKETS = ON
        CONNECTIONS = 8
        NETWORK PRINTERS = 3
        FIRST NETWORK DRIVE = F
    ;   NAME CONTEXT = "o=widgetco"
        MESSAGE LEVEL = 3
        SIGNATURE LEVEL = 0
```

Notice that in this version of the file, several items are remarked out that weren't in the first file. At the same time, the items remarked out in the first file are loaded in this file. For instance, the SECURITY.VLM, NDS.VLM, and RSA.VLM modules are not loaded. The PREFERRED TREE= statement is bypassed, as is the NAME CONTEXT= statement. Since these modules and statements are directly related to logging in as a Directory client, they aren't necessary for bindery client logins.

In both sample files, you could remark out lines that aren't necessary for the VLM client software to work. In newer versions of the VLMs, remarking out or eliminating these lines can provide memory gains as well as possible performance enhancements. When you set up and use the VLM client software, be sure to thoroughly read the documentation that comes with the software and only load those VLM modules that you absolutely need. The documentation also explains which parameters can be used to optimize the VLM performance.

Example 3

Here is an example of a NET.CFG file optimized for performance using various NET.CFG parameters. The following file is for logging into a NetWare 4 network as an NDS client:

```
Link Driver NE2000
     INT 3
     PORT 300
     FRAME Ethernet_802.2
SHOW DOTS ON
NETWARE DOS REQUESTER
     USE DEFAULTS = OFF
     VLM = CONN.VLM
     VLM = IPXNCP.VLM
     VLM = TRAN.VLM
     VLM = SECURITY.VLM
     VLM = NDS.VLM
     VLM = RSA.VLM
     VLM = NWP.VLM
     VLM = FIO.VLM
     VLM = GENERAL.VLM
     VLM = REDIR.VLM
     VLM = PRINT.VLM
     VLM = AUTO.VLM
     PREFERRED TREE = WIDGETCO
     AUTO RETRY = 10
     VLM STACK SWITCH = ON
     CHECKSUM = 0
     PB BUFFERS = 3
     LARGE INTERNET PACKETS = ON
     CONNECTIONS = 20
     NETWORK PRINTERS = 3
     FIRST NETWORK DRIVE = F
```

```
SIGNATURE LEVEL = 0
LOAD LOW CONN TABLE = ON
LOAD LOW IPXNCP = ON
CACHE WRITES = ON
```

In this example, only the necessary VLM modules are loaded. Notice BIND.VLM and NETX.VLM are not in the load list. The reason they are not loaded is the existence of the "USE DEFAULTS = OFF" statement at the top of the list right under the NetWare DOS Requester heading. By default, the VLM.EXE module loads all of the VLM modules in its default list (whether they are needed or not) unless the USE DEFAULTS = OFF statement is inserted in the proper location in the NET.CFG file, and you specify which modules you want to load. If this statement is missing, you get warnings about modules that are not in the list, but all of the default VLMs will load.

Also notice the PREFERRED SERVER = statement is missing from this NET.CFG file. Since this file is for a Directory Services login, we use the PREFERRED TREE = statement as a means of directing the client software to the Directory tree to which we want to login.

The rest of the statements listed in the NET.CFG file are common parameters used to customize the client software to fit the user's personal preferences. It's not necessary to discuss those here, as they are documented in both the NetWare 4 documentation and in the *NetWare Application Notes*. The latest version of the VLM client software should also have documentation included with it. As of this writing, the client software and related files can be downloaded from Novell's NetWire Forum on CompuServe (**GO NETWIRE**).

Example 4

The following NET.CFG file is optimized for a bindery-based login:

```
Link Driver NE2000
      INT 3
      PORT 300
      FRAME Ethernet_802.2

SHOW DOTS ON
NETWARE DOS REQUESTER
      USE DEFAULTS = OFF
      VLM = CONN.VLM
      VLM = IPXNCP.VLM
      VLM = TRAN.VLM
      VLM = BIND.VLM
      VLM = NWP.VLM
      VLM = FIO.VLM
      VLM = GENERAL.VLM
      VLM = REDIR.VLM
      VLM = PRINT.VLM
      VLM = NETX.VLM
      VLM = AUTO.VLM
      PREFERRED SERVER = WIDGETMAN
      BIND RECONNECT = ON
      AUTO RETRY = 30
      LOAD CONN TABLE LOW = ON
      LOAD IPXNCP TABLE LOW = ON
      CHECKSUM = 0
      PB BUFFERS = 3
      LARGE INTERNET PACKETS = ON
      NETWORK PRINTERS = 3
      FIRST NETWORK DRIVE = F
      MESSAGE LEVEL = 3
      SIGNATURE LEVEL = 0
```

Again, only the necessary VLM modules are loaded. Notice that SECU-RITY.VLM, NDS.VLM, and RSA.VLM are not in the list. Since the USE DEFAULTS = OFF line is placed correctly in the file, only the modules listed will load.

The rest of the parameter statements listed in the NET.CFG file are common parameters used to customize the client software to fit the user's personal preferences. They are documented in both the NetWare 4 documentation and in the *NetWare Application Notes*.

Logging In and Using the Client Utilities

After installing and configuring you VLM client software, you are ready to login to your network. Remember that in NetWare 4 you no longer login to a file server. Instead, you login to the network. Also consider that different users access network services in different ways.

Logging into the correct Directory tree

If you only have one Directory tree for your entire network, this step is simple. However, if you have created more than one Directory tree to which users can login, the users have to specify to which tree they want to login. It is easiest to add the PREFERRED TREE = *treename* statement in users' NET.CFG files to designate the correct default tree. This entry automatically places users in their home Directory tree where they login, which is usually where they perform their primary tasks and have access to their most frequently used network resources.

Setting up the correct name context

Once you have designated the proper tree for your users to login, you need to specify the proper context for where the user will login. This is accomplished by setting the NAME CONTEXT = *context path* statement in the users' NET.CFG files. Setting this parameter provides a set point of entry into the Directory tree where the user has access.

When this statement is entered correctly in the NET.CFG file, the user simply types **LOGIN** *username* and presses **Enter** to login to the network. This is much easier than having to manually type out the proper context. If users need to login at a different access point in the Directory tree, they can still do that by typing out the exact context in the LOGIN command.

To clarify this concept, think of an NDS user's default Directory tree and context as a mailing address for that user. Here is how the NDS terms relate to this mailing address analogy:

- *CN = Common Name.* The user's name.

- *OU = Organizational Unit.* The street address or PO Box number, apartment or suite number, and city where the user resides (There can be more than one OU in a context).

- *O = Organization.* The user's state and ZIP code.

Just as in a standard mailing address, these different elements must be ordered properly to ensure accurate mail delivery. In Directory Services, the proper order for the name context is as follows:

1. Common Name (CN)

2. Organizational Unit(s) (OUs)

3. Organization (O)

In the simplest possible tree, there will be only a Common Name and an Organization. You can set up any number of Organizational Units in your tree. However, keep in mind the more levels you set up, the more complex your Directory will be to use and administer.

Here is a sample NDS context for user GHERBON:

- *CN=GHERBON* (the user's login name)

- *OU=SALES* (the container representing the user's department)

- *OU=CODY* (the container representing the user's division)

- *O=WIDGETCO* (the top container representing the user's company name)

In writing out the name context for the above example, the context string would be:

```
CN=GHERBON.OU=SALES.OU=CODY.O=WIDGETCO
```

This NDS context defines how the user GHERBON has access to the Directory tree and to its resources. Remember that a user's Common Name (CN) is always first in the string and the Organization (O) is always last.

When you designate the context in the NET.CFG file with the NAME CONTEXT = parameter, users don't have to type out the proper context every time they need to login. For the example above, the NAME CONTEXT = line in GHERBON's NET.CFG file would look like this:

```
NAME CONTEXT = "OU=SALES.OU=CODY.O=WIDGETCO"
```

The context string itself must be enclosed in quotes. This parameter sets the VLM client software to the proper context in the Directory tree. Thus when user GHERBON logs in, he only has to type **login gherbon** at the network prompt and press **Enter.**

This command automatically places the user's Common Name (GHERBON) at the beginning of the Directory tree context. This places the user in the proper context to login to the Directory and access the resources and services that he has rights to in this part of the Directory tree. Once this is done, the user can use the NetWare utilities and login script drive mappings to access all his resources.

For example, if GHERBON logs in this way and types **whoami** and presses **Enter,** he sees something similar to the following:

```
Current Tree: WIDGETCO
Complete Name:
CN=GHERBON.OU=SALES.OU=CODY.O=WIDGETCO
```

If you have users that need easy access to different parts (contexts) of the Directory tree, these users can use the NetWare CX (Change Context) command to change to the Directory tree context they need to access.

An example of this situation would be if user GHERBON needed to login to a second Directory tree after he has either logged into the primary location in the Directory tree or booted his computer (which activates the NET.CFG settings). The VLM software still recognizes OU=SALES.OU= CODY.O=WIDGETCO as the current context. However, if user GHERBON knows the name of the second Directory tree (WIDGETMAN, for example), he can use the LOGIN *treename/username* /TR command by typing **login widgetman/gherbon/tr** and pressing **Enter.**

If GHERBON happens to know his entire context within the new Directory tree, he can use the CX command to change directly to that context in the new Directory tree. This would be accomplished by typing **cx .sales_sw.sales.widgetman** and pressing **Enter.**

The leading period in this example clears the Directory context information stored in the VLM client software. By implementing this command, you are specifying a completely new Directory context, not just supplying a partial name dependent on information stored in the VLM client software. When using this command, user GHERBON can then login by simply typing **login gherbon** and pressing **Enter.**

He will be prompted to enter his password for the second Directory tree.

NetWare 4 also allows the use of partial names to move to different areas (contexts) in the Directory tree. For example, if user GHERBON is working in the context CN=GHERBON.OU=SALES_SW.OU=SALES.WIDGET-MAN and wants to work from the ACCOUNTING Organizational Unit residing at the same level as SALES_SW, he can move to that context by typing **cx ou=accounting.** and pressing **Enter.**

Note that the trailing period (at the end of ACCOUNTING) removes the first piece (OU=SALES_SW) from GHERBON's current Directory context and adds OU=ACCOUNTING to produce

```
OU=ACCOUNTING.OU=SALES.O=WIDGETMAN
```

as the new context. If GHERBON types **whoami** and presses **Enter** after completing this command, he sees the following:

```
Current Tree: WIDGETMAN
Complete Name:
CN=GHERBON.OU=ACCOUNTING.OU=SALES.O=WIDGETMAN
```

In most circumstances, Directory tree contexts probably won't be this complex. You might have a Directory tree context that consists only of an Organization (O). Using the CONTEXT NAME = and the TREE NAME = parameters in the NET.CFG file makes it a lot easier for your users to get into the Directory tree at the proper location.

You can use NAME CONTEXT = "[Root]" if you don't want to limit your users to a specified O or OU. Using "[Root]" for this parameter can bypass certain anomalies in the login process. If this is the setting you are using for your name context, you can then specify the proper Organizational Unit (OU) as well as your proper context name when you login.

If you know the name of a server in your context, you can also use the server name to login to the correct context. For example, if server Widget is in the same context as User object GHERBON is defined in, he could type **login widget/gherbon** and press **Enter** to login to that context. In this case, the user initially logs in at the root, then moves to the context where the server is located.

It is also important to note that the VLM client software does not verify that the context specified in the NAME CONTEXT = parameter actually exists in the Directory tree. If your actual Directory context differs from what you specify in the aforementioned parameter, the name context the VLM client software recognizes will be the one that is set in your parameter (whether it exists or not). This can be quite confusing to users and makes it extremely hard for them to login to the network. Be sure to set the *correct* context in the NET.CFG file.

Let's look at an example of the situation described above. If you were to set the NAME CONTEXT = "O=DIDGETMAN" in your NET.CFG and you then try to login as user ADMIN, the Common Name ADMIN is placed before O=DIDGETMAN, giving you CN=ADMIN.O=DIDGETMAN. This is the entry that is passed to Directory Services for authentication. However, if DIDGETMAN is not a valid Organization container, NDS returns the message *Access Denied* and you won't be authenticated.

Remember your Common Name is always placed before the context specified in the VLM client software. Be sure to carefully enter the correct information in the NAME CONTEXT = statement in the NET.CFG file. Also be sure to use the correct Common Names when logging in.

Other LOGIN variations

Following are some other helpful variations on the LOGIN command using different parameters:

- LOGIN *servername/username* /NS attaches you to the specified server, but does not run the login script. (This works the same as ATTACH in earlier versions of

NetWare. However, you can still use the ATTACH command in login scripts.)

- LOGIN *username* /B enacts a bindery emulation login process from NetWare 4. This is useful if you need to login to a bindery-based server.

Using the NetWare CX command

The NetWare CX command is useful for finding out where you are in the Directory tree, as well as for navigating around the different contexts in the Directory. Here are some examples of how you can use the CX command with its different parameters:

- CX shows you your current context in the Directory tree.

- CX /T lets you view the Directory tree below your current location.

- CX /T /A allows you to view all the objects that are defined at or below your current context location.

- CX /R takes you to the [Root] of the Directory tree.

- CX /HELP displays help information for the CX command.

Remember, what you can see using the CX command is limited by what rights you have at the [Root] and at the various levels of the Directory tree. Two users might run CX from the same Directory context, yet be able to see completely different resources or services.

Besides using the CX command, you can use the NetWare WHOAMI command to view the entire Directory tree context, as well as the parts of the Directory to which you have proper rights.

This is by no means a complete discussion of what you can do with the NetWare CX command. Play around with it and find out what it can do!

197

Using the NetWare NLIST utility

The NetWare NLIST utility allows you to view available resources in the Directory from your Directory tree context. Numerous parameters can be used with NLIST to see a variety of different things in the Directory. I discuss several of these parameter variations to provide simple examples of how to access helpful information.

N O T E

As you use NLIST (and similar commands), bear in mind that what you will see is limited by the rights you have at each level of the Directory and at the [Root]. Also be aware that what you see is also dependent upon the amount of information defined for each of the NDS objects through the NETADMIN or NWAdmin utilities.

- NLIST USER = GHERBON /D displays all of the property information associated with the specified user including login script, telephone numbers, e-mail address, and so on (if this information has been entered for this User object.)

- NLIST PRINTER /S searches your local Directory context and its subcontainers for printers.

- NLIST PRINTER /CO "." /S lets you see what printers are above you in the Directory tree context (to which you have the proper rights).

- NLIST /TREE = * allows you to see all of the Directory trees available to you on the internetwork.

- NLIST SERVER /B lets you see all bindery-based servers. This is the NetWare 4 equivalent of the SLIST command.

- NLIST SERVER WHERE "VERSION" = 4.* lists all servers running NetWare 4.

- NLIST SERVER = *servername* /A lets you find out if the specified server is active.

- NLIST USER /A displays a list of all currently logged in users.

NetWare 4 Directory Services allows you the capability of setting up NDS objects so other NDS objects (such as users) can see various information about the NDS objects, such as users' phone numbers and e-mail addresses. While NetWare 4 provides this flexibility, not everyone will set up their Directory objects with this much information. Keep this in mind when using NLIST and other commands to find out what is available to you in the Directory tree.

Summary

This chapter has provided an overview of how the NetWare DOS Requester (VLM) client software works and how to use it to login to NetWare Directory Services. It also contains information about a few of the NetWare commands you can use to navigate around the Directory. We have given several specific examples of NET.CFG files that can be used with the VLM client software. You will have to experiment and find out what works best for your particular situation.

Assigning NDS Security

This chapter discusses the assignment of different security rights. We have already discussed access control and the differences between object and property rights in previous chapters. Many of the necessary rights are provided by the NetWare 4 defaults. The defaults are designed to work for most situations where User objects reside in the same container as the resources they access the most. By default, users created in the same container as a NetWare 4 server can login and use the other system resources defined in that container.

However, there may be cases where it is necessary to assign additional rights beyond those given by default. These include the following circumstances:

- When profile login scripts are assigned to users.

- When Directory map objects are created.

- When special types of users are established (such as e-mail database administrators).

- When the tree's administration is divided among two or more individuals.

- When you allow users to login as Aliases in containers other than those that contain their original user object.

Assigning NDS Rights for the Use of Profile Login Scripts

First let's take a look at assigning rights when profile login scripts are assigned to users. A profile login script is a new type of login script introduced in NetWare 4. Profile login scripts set up a common working environment for multiple users that reside in the same container. In other words, this is a "shared" login script that can be used by anyone that has the proper rights assigned to them. (They need to be able to read the login script property of the profile object.)

If all users needing to use the profile login script reside in the same container as the Profile object, an additional assignment of rights is not required. In some cases, users who need to use a common profile script reside in different containers, and thus require an additional rights assignment. It is this group we focus on here.

To assign the necessary additional rights to users who reside in different containers but need to use a common profile login script, complete the following steps:

1. Create the necessary Profile object.

2. Fill in the Profile Login Script property for the Profile object.

3. Assign the Profile Login Script as the login script for each individual user that needs to run it.

4. Make each user of the Profile Login Script a trustee by granting them both the Browse [B] object right and the Read [R] property right for the login script.

This allows all users assigned those rights to use the specified profile login script. While these steps are simple, they are important for providing the users the required access, while at the same time preventing use by those who do not need access to the specified profile login script.

Assigning Rights for Directory Map Objects

Directory Map objects are new in NetWare 4 and provide greater flexibility than the drive mappings used in bindery-based versions of NetWare. Directory Map objects map a pointer to a file system, rather than a specific directory. Thus to use a Directory Map object, users must have the proper rights to allow them to read the properties that point to the actual directory. Each user that uses Directory Map objects must have the Read [R] All Properties assignment to the specified Directory Map object.

Setting Up Specialized Administrators

It may be useful to create specialized users to administer various facets of your network. I'll use an e-mail administrator as an example. Such a situation requires special rights that you will want to assign carefully. Choose someone you trust for this position, as they will be granted some farily powerful rights. Setting up an Organizational Role for these functions may not be wise, because of the rights that must be granted to this individual.

Since the e-mail administrator will be managing properties of individual User objects, only selected individuals should receive this assignment. You cannot assign the administrator position to a specified group of users because he or she would be managing the group object properties rather than the individual user objects. You should not assign rights to the e-mail administrator using the All Properties selection, as that includes far too many rights (including rights to the ACL property).

203

The e-mail administrator would typically assign the following rights for each of the individual user objects he or she is responsible for:

E-mail address	[R W] Read and Write
Address	[R W] Read and Write
Phone number	[R W] Read and Write
FAX number	[R W] Read and Write

It is important to understand the ramifications of assigning the [R W] rights using the All Properties option. All Properties includes the object ACL property. The [W] right to an object's ACL property controls who can change trustee assignments to that particular object. This situation would be similar to a user having the Access Control file system right to a file system directory. A user that has this right can change other users' rights to the specified directory. This is also the case with someone that has the [W] right to the ACL property. They can also assign other users rights to the directory as well.

If you make the above rights assignment, even by oversight, the e-mail administrator would have more rights than originally intended or needed. Again, be careful when assigning rights such as these. Be sure you fully understand all implications prior to making the assignment, not after the fact when damage may have already been done.

Dividing Subtree Administration Duties

In NetWare 4, an important aspect of administration is how the administrative duties are split up. In some cases (such as small networks or networks where all objects reside in the same container), it may make sense to have one ADMIN for the entire network. However, most network environments will probably be managed more effectively by using a different ADMIN for each branch of the Directory tree.

Currently there are two schools of thought when dividing administration duties: Use one administrator per branch, or use an assistant administrator who will mange a "workgroup." The type that is best for your network environment will probably be dictated by your organization's specific security needs.

Let's look at both types of Directory administration and try to provide some insight on which type of administrator would work best for your needs. First we'll look at the single-administrator approach.

Single administrator NDS management scheme

The use of a single administrator for a branch of the tree seems to be the most prevalent method of Directory management currently in use. With this method, you assign only one user with ADMIN rights to a particular branch of your Directory tree. This method is the most secure one, as no one has total control of the entire network. While it is unlikely that any one person (if given authority over the entire Directory) will try to "take over" the network and hold it hostage, there are reported cases of this happening.

The single-administrator method might be required in a government or government contractor environment. If the single Admin approach is the one being used in the aforementioned environments, it might be necessary to cut off the rights inherited by the original Admin user (the one created at installation time, if different than the Admin that is managing the specific section of the tree).

To ensure the new Admin has the necessary rights to manage the section of the tree, and to cut off the original Admin's rights to the specified section of the Directory tree, complete the following steps.

1. Assign user Teri an explicit trustee assignment to OU=SALES of [SBCDR] object rights and [SRCWA] property rights.

Make sure all rights are assigned (not just the [S] right) to ensure complete branch administration is possible even if the [S] right is filtered out by an Inherited Rights Filter (IRF).

2. Revoke all inherited rights to ensure the original Admin cannot inherit rights to the OU=SALES area of the Directory tree. This is accomplished by setting the IRF to [B] object rights and the [R] property rights.

    Be sure you do not revoke the Browse object right. If you do, your users will not be able to see that part of the tree.

3. Remove all trustee assignments the original Admin user had to OU=SALES.

4. Be sure Teri has [S] object rights to herself. Once this is done, remove any trustee assignments to CN=Teri that the original Admin was given. This prevents the original Admin from restricting your new Admin's rights.

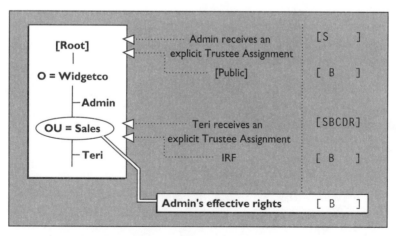

Figure 11-1. Setting up a single administrator for part of the tree.

Remember, you must assign explicit trustee assignments that include the [S] right before revoking the general [S] right using the IRF. The NetWare 4 utilities do not let you revoke the [S] right without having made explicit trustee assignments that include the [S] right.

However, you still need to be careful because you can lose control of a branch of the tree if you delete the only user that has the [S] right in an explicit trustee assignment. Thus, it is important to set up your Directory security so if any of your branch administrators leave your company under less than favorable circumstances, you can still manage the resources in that branch of the tree.

Workgroup manager NDS management scheme

It is possibile your company or organization may need central administration to provide Directory security. At the same time, you may also need to provide Directory management at the department or workgroup level. As shown in the single administrator example above, you can cut off administrative control of a branch from the central administrator. With this is mind, be sure you set up security so that you can still manage any branch of your tree that was managed by an administrator who left your company under unfavorable circumstances.

To ensure administrative control is not cut off from any branches of your Directory tree, complete the following steps:

1. Assign user Teri an explicit trustee assignment to OU=SALES that includes the following rights: the [BCDR] object rights, the [RCWA] All Properties rights, and the [RC] ACL property rights.

   Note here that reassignment of ACL property rights overrides the rights assigned to All Properties rights. This prevents CN=Teri from modifying the trustee assignments to OU=SALES and thus preventing her from deleting anyone (including herself) from the ACL.

2. Ensure that your central Admin has an explicit trustee assignment to OU=SALES by assigning her the following rights: CN=Admin to OU=SALES the [SBCDR] object rights and the [SRCWA] all properties rights.

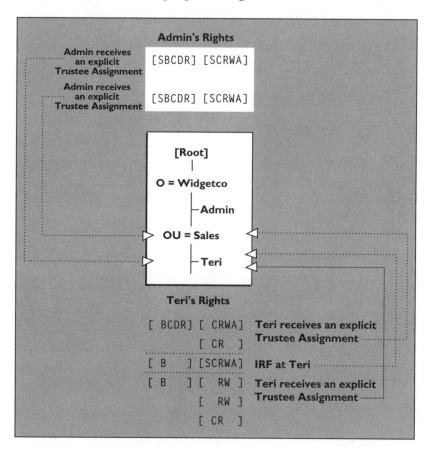

Admin's Rights

Admin receives an explicit Trustee Assignment — [SBCDR] [SCRWA]

Admin receives an explicit Trustee Assignment — [SBCDR] [SCRWA]

[Root]
|
O = Widgetco
|
├─Admin
|
OU = Sales
|
├─Teri

Teri's Rights

[BCDR] [CRWA]	Teri receives an explicit Trustee Assignment
[CR]	
[B] [SCRWA]	IRF at Teri
[B] [RW]	Teri receives an explicit Trustee Assignment
[RW]	
[CR]	

Figure 11-2. Assigning a workgroup manager for a department.

3. Assign your central Admin an explicit trustee assignment to CN=Teri by assigning her the following rights: CN=Admin to CN=Teri the [SBCDR] object rights and the [SRCWA] all properties rights.

4. Be sure to revoke all inherited rights except the Browse right [B] to object CN=Teri so Teri cannot inherit rights to manage herself. Do this by assigning the following IRF: IRF [B] object rights only.

5. Reassign the following rights Teri has to herself, so she cannot assign herself more rights:

CN=Teri to CN=Teri   [B   ] object rights

[R W] Login script property

[R W] Print job configuration

[RC] ACL property

This management scheme works because Teri can manage this branch of the tree, while at the same time she cannot change trustee assignments in the OU=SALES because her access has been restricted from the OU=SALES container's ACL property.

Security for Alias Logins

NDS users can be assigned Alias objects to allow them easier access to different parts of the Directory. When users have an Alias object created for them, they can login as their Alias. However, every time a user logs in as an Alias object, the system login script belonging to the container in which the Alias resides is used, rather than that of the container where the user's "real" user object resides.

Whenever you create a user Alias in a different container than the original user object, you must assign the Alias object the proper rights to run the new container's login script. This is a simple task, and can be accomplished by assigning the Alias object the Read [R] right to the login script property of the container where the Alias resides.

Necessary NDS Rights for Printing

Printing in NetWare 4 is managed quite similarly to how it was managed in NetWare 3.11: through operators and users. Thus NetWare 4 printing does not require any rights. However, to manage a NetWare 4 print server, you must be a print server operator. To manage print queues, you must be a print queue operator. Likewise, you must be a print queue user to print to a printer or to a print queue.

By default, NetWare 4 makes the container the print queue is created in a print queue user. Thus every user who resides in that container can print to the queues in their own containers without individual designation as print queue users.

Assigning Additional Rights to the NetWare 4 File System

Assigning additional file system rights in NetWare 4 is similar to doing so in previous versions of NetWare. It is still necessary for the file system administrator to assign additional file system rights for the following:

- Applications and data files that users need to access.

- Users who reside in a different context than the file server and thus do not inherit file system rights to SYS:PUBLIC.

Applications and data files

Every time a new application is installed on the server, you must assign the proper file-system rights so users can access the applications. Users also need a separate area (such as a home directory) where they can store and access their data files.

Users residing in a different context than the server

Users who reside in the same container as the server are assigned—by default—the Read and File Scan rights for SYS:PUBLIC. However, any users created outside of the container where the server resides do not inherit these rights. If this situation exists in your network environment, the file-system rights mentioned above (Read and File Scan) must be assigned elsewhere for those users to execute the drive mappings of the default login script. If the user's do not have the proper file-system rights to SYS:PUBLIC, the following error message is apt to appear:

```
Current drive is not valid>
```

This problem also occurs whenever users attach to servers that reside outside of the user's container. When login script drive mappings (such as in the default login script) do not specify the specific server, NetWare attempts to map the drives to the file server the user attached to when logging in. However, this could be a different server than desired, and the mapping operation will fail. Thus, it is important to specify all necessary information in the drive mappings, and to assign the proper rights wherever needed.

Where to Assign Rights

With NetWare 4 you are given greater flexibility with rights assignments. You can now assign rights to containers, groups, Organizational Roles, users, and the [Public] trustee. This gives you the option of assigning rights where they best fit your specific needs.

[Root] object

In a small or simple network environment it is quite possible that all your users may need access to all of your servers. If this is the case, you can assign file system rights to SYS:PUBLIC at the [Root] object. You can also assign rights to commonly used applications such as WordPerfect, Paradox, or Quattro Pro to the [Root] object. By assigning these rights to the [Root] object, all users inherit these rights. Assigning rights at the [Root] is the simplest way of assigning rights to all users, and allows users to easily access and run common applications from different servers when their primary server is off-line.

You might also want to consider assigning file system rights at the [Root] object level if you have numerous users who travel frequently from site to site. This allows those users to easily map to and run local applications rather than making them use their applications over a wide area network (WAN).

However, you should assign rights at the [Root] object level carefully. Remember, all rights assigned to the [Root] object are inherited by *all* users. Most rights are management rights and are not needed by most users (other than your administrator). The one right that should be assigned at the [Root] is Browse. The Browse right allows your users to see the other objects that reside in your tree. The Browse right is automatically assigned to the [Root] during server installation when the [Public] trustee is assigned.

Organization objects

NetWare 4 allows you to assign rights to a specified Organization object. Note that assigning rights to the organization object is quite similar to when you assign them at the [Root] level. However, assigning rights to an Organization object allows you more specific control than assigning rights at the [Root] level.

For example, if you had three different Organization objects (such as US, UK, and Jamaica), you may need to assign rights to your users in the O=Jamaica that aren't needed by your other Organization objects. This allows you to segregate these rights by Organization, rather that granting them to everyone in your entire company. This also provides a somewhat higher level of security than assigning rights at the [Root] level.

 All NDS and file-system rights are assigned to a container are inherited by all users in that container. This applies to Organizational Unit container objects as well as Organization container objects.

N O T E

Assigning rights to containers is an easy way to assign rights to a large group of users. However, because all rights assigned to a container are inherited by all users in that container, be careful you do not assign unnecessary rights to containers.

Organizational Unit objects

The flexibility provided by assigning rights at the Organizational Unit object level makes this the most useful container level to assign rights. For departments or workgroups, assigning file system rights at the OU level provide common rights for servers in the OU. It also allows you to assign rights to data files and applications closer to your User objects. This provides greater of security.

For example, your regional sales departments (SALES_SW and SALES_NE) could share contact database applications if the proper rights assignments are made to the OU=SALES Organizational Unit object since each department has its own OU under the parent Organizational Unit of OU=SALES

Again, you should carefully consider whether you really want to assign rights to *everyone* who resides in the specified Organizational Unit before assigning rights in this manner.

213

NDS Profiles and Directory Maps

Although both of these objects have a property called "Rights to the File System," you should never assign file system rights to either of these objects in this manner. If you assign rights in this manner are not inherited by users that use the Profile Login Script or by those that map to the Directory Map object. Assigning rights to these objects in this manner has no affect on the file-system rights of the user.

Group or Organizational Role

Assigning rights at the Group or Organizational Role level is an option you might want to use if you are unable to assign rights at the container level due to data sensitivity. Assigning file-system rights to these objects is also a simple and practical solution for those circumstances where you have database or sensitive application servers where only certain a certain user or users need access to the file system on those servers. The only thing to be aware of here is that you must specifically add the users who need access to the specified Group or Organizational Role, and you must delete any users who reside in these objects that you do not want to have the rights assigned to.

Summary

While assigning security is a new and somewhat difficult concept to grasp, its successful implementation provides improved network management and easier administration. Take the time to become familiar with the concepts of security. Use this chapter as a guide to plan and implement security for your network environment. Future releases of NetWare 4 will provide additional utilities to enhance your use and administration of security.

Section 3

Maintaining NetWare Directory Services

Managing NDS Objects

This chapter discusses the NetWare 4 administration utilities: NETADMIN (text based) and NWAdmin (GUI based). These two utilities create and manage NDS objects in the Directory tree. Both provide options that make NDS object creation and administration fairly simple and straightforward. You can use whichever utility best suits your needs.

Either utility can be used to perform the following managerial tasks for NDS objects:

- Create NDS objects, including Users, Groups, Organizational Roles, and Profiles.

- Move, rename, or delete NDS objects.

- Change the properties of an NDS object.

- Search for NDS objects.

To install the NetWare 4 administration utilities, refer to the documentation that came with your NetWare operating system software.

N O T E The NetWare Administrator utilities deal only with NDS object and property rights. Do not use either NETADMIN or NWAdmin to assign file system directory and file rights; there are other utilities to do that. See your NetWare 4 documentation for details.

Rights Necessary to Manage Objects

Before explaining how to use NETADMIN or NWAdmin to accomplish the tasks listed above, I will discuss what rights are needed to make changes to the NDS database and manage the objects that reside in the Directory tree. The administrative utilities were designed to be used by the User object Admin (or by a person who holds the Admin rights for a particular branch of the tree). Initially, user Admin has all rights to all objects in the entire Directory tree. If you have designated any users as Admins for other parts of the tree, you must assign them the proper access and managerial rights to that section of the tree.

As explained in previous chapters, granting NDS object rights to another object is referred to as making a trustee assignment. An NDS object given a trustee assignment to another object becomes a trustee of that object. For example, if you grant a User object (such as KNEFF) rights to a container (such as SALES_SW), user KNEFF becomes a trustee of that container. A list of all trustee assignments is kept in each object's Access Control List (ACL) property.

To give you more flexibility and control over your Directory tree, NetWare 4 allows you to assign separately NDS object and property rights. NDS object rights determine what trustees are allowed to do with a specific object as a single item in the Directory tree. NDS trustee assignments usually don't allow the trustee of an NDS object to gain access to the information stored in the object's properties, unless the Supervisor right is granted to the trustee.

NDS Object Rights

Browse   See an object in the Directory tree, or when performing a search for a value that matches the object.

Create   Create a new object in a specified container object in the tree.

Delete   Delete an object from the tree (leaf object or empty container object).

Rename   Change an object's name (leaf only).

Supervisor   Grant *all* rights to an NDS object and all of its properties.

NDS Property Rights

Read   See or "read" the value of a specified property (includes the Compare right).

Write   Add, remove, or change any of a property's values (includes the Add or Delete Self right).

Compare   Allow the comparison of any property's value to that of any existing property value (returns True or False).

Add or Delete Self Allow a trustee to add or delete itself as one of a property's values, without being able to change any other values of the property.

Supervisor   Grant *all* rights to an object's properties.

Figure 12-1. NDS rights needed to perform administrative tasks in NetWare 4.

Any object that has been granted sufficient rights can use the NetWare 4 administration utilities to make trustee assignments. However, the rights needed are different for various NDS trustee assignments. Figure 12-1 gives a quick review of what rights are needed to perform various managerial functions.

Now that you know which NDS object and property rights are needed, we can discuss the actual process of creating and maintaining NDS objects using NETADMIN and NWAdmin. (Chapter 2 discusses the types of NDS container and leaf objects available in NetWare 4.)

Using the NETADMIN Utility

NETADMIN is a text-based network administration utility included with NetWare 4. This utility is accessed by logging in at a DOS client workstation and typing **NETADMIN** at the command line to start the utility. The main NETADMIN screen is displayed, as shown in Figure 12-2.

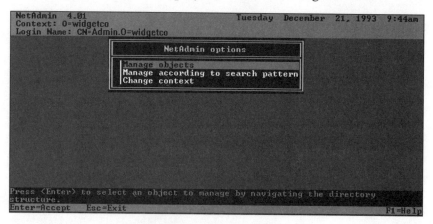

Figure 12-2. NETADMIN's main screen.

The NETADMIN screen displays information that will be helpful as you use the utility. Notice the following elements in particular:

- The first line (at the top of the screen) gives the name and version number of the utility, along with the current date and time.

- The second line displays the current NDS Directory context. It's similar to a file system directory path. You can view or modify only those objects residing in the specified container. The context information changes as you move through the Directory tree using the Browser.

- The third line indicates your login name. This information can be useful when assigning object trustee rights. It is also helpful if you routinely login using different names to accomplish different tasks. For instance, GHerbon might log in as Admin to perform management functions for an entire branch of the tree. At other times he may just login as himself and browse those things to which User object GHERBON has specific rights. This line remains constant throughout the current session.

Now look at the three lines at the bottom of the NETADMIN screen. These lines provide information about what options are available for every screen in the utility.

- The very bottom line of the screen provides a list of the currently active function keys. These are consistent throughout the NetWare 4 text-based utilities. If more function keys are active than can be listed on the bottom line, a notation in the lower-right corner states that you can press the **Alt+F1** key combination to see more active function keys.

- The two lines directly above the bottom line contain summarized information of what actions you can perform in the current screen. This is what Novell refers to as Quick

Help. Each screen in the NetWare text-based utilities provides information to that screen. You can also press the **F1**
key at any time to get context-sensitive help for the field
with which you are currently working.

You should become familiar with the three options available from the
main screen:

1. The *Manage objects* option is the one you will use the
   most. Selecting this option brings up the Browser portion
   of the NETADMIN utility. You'll use the Browser exten-
   sively to locate and view the objects in each container.

2. The *Manage according to search pattern* option is used
   when you want to manage only objects of a specific class
   or objects that match certain search patterns.

3. The *Change context* option allows you to change your
   context in the Directory tree.

Before proceeding further, let's look more closely at NETADMIN's
Browser function.

The NETADMIN Browser

The Browser is the part of the NETADMIN utility that allows you to
locate objects in the Directory tree. Using the Browser, you can move
around the NDS tree by selecting parent and child container objects. (The
Context displayed on line two is updated as you move through the tree.)
Once you arrive at the proper container, you can then add, delete, or edit
objects in that container.

NETADMIN limits you to seeing the contents of *one* Directory
tree context (or container) at a time. The NWAdmin utility
shows the tree in graphical form so you can see the entire hierarchy of containers and move more quickly to the one you want.

222

The Browser is a very handy tool. After installing NetWare 4, you can use the Browser to make sure the NDS objects that were supposed to be created by the INSTALL program were actually created.

Now that you have a pretty good feel for the screen layout of NETADMIN, we can explain how to actually use the utility.

Creating a container object using NETADMIN

In working with the NDS database, the logical starting point is to create any necessary container objects. When creating new NDS objects, remember these simple rules:

- Every Directory tree is required to have a [Root] (the topmost object in the tree) and at least one Organization (O) container object directly beneath the [Root].

- You can create as many Organizational Unit (OU) container objects as you need. OUs must be at least one level lower than Os.

- Container objects can contain leaf objects and other container objects. Leaf objects cannot hold any other objects of any kind.

- Follow naming standards and restrictions for NDS object names. (For specific information on object naming restrictions, see Appendix A.)

N O T E   The [Root] object at the top of the Directory tree is created by default during the NetWare 4 installation process, so you don't need to worry about creating it. Other O and OU container objects may have been created during installation as well.

With these rules in mind, let's create an OU container object in NETADMIN. Note that we will also create a User_Template object in the OU.

User_Templates simplify the creation of User objects by eliminating the need to manually enter all information for new users added to an OU.

1. If you haven't already done so, start NETADMIN by logging in at a DOS client workstation. At the command line, type **NETADMIN**, and then press **Enter**.

   Remember to login as Admin or some other User object that has rights to manage your portion of the Directory tree.

2. Highlight the **Manage objects** option and press **Enter**.

3. If necessary, use the Browser function to get to the proper context in which you want to create the container object. Selecting the .. *(parent)* entry moves you up one level in the tree.

Always double check the second line of the screen to make sure you are in the right context before creating new objects. Otherwise you may inadvertently create them at the wrong place in the tree.

4. Once you are in the right context, press **Ins** to bring up the Object, Class list.

5. Since you are creating an OU, scroll through the items listed until **Organizational Unit** is highlighted. Press **Enter** to accept this choice.

6. In the *Create object Organizational Unit* window, type the name you want for your new OU next to *New name*: and press **Enter**.

7. In the *Create User_Template?* field, answer **Yes** to create a User_Template object in the new container. If you do not want to do this, leave it set to No.

8. Press **F10** to create the new OU.

9. The *Create another?* prompt is displayed. To create another container object, answer **Yes** and repeat the process described above. If you are finished creating containers in this context, answer **No** to the prompt.

Setting up User_Templates

Before creating users in the new container, you need to set up the User_Template you created so it contains the common (default) properties you want all users in this container to have.

N O T E You can create a User_Template object when you add a new container. When you answered Yes in the Create User_Template? field, a User object with the name USER_TEMPLATE was created in the container. For container objects created by the INSTALL NLM, you must manually create User_Template objects.

Whenever you create new User objects, you can use NETADMIN to copy properties from the nearest User_Template object. NETADMIN searches the current context for the User_Template object. If one cannot be found in the current context, NETADMIN searches the parent contexts until a User_Template object is found, or until the utility reaches the top of the Directory tree.

You need to modify the properties of the User_Template in your new container so you have something to copy to new users. Do this as follows:

1. While in the Browser portion of NETADMIN, make sure the second line at the top of the screen displays the correct context. If not, move to the container you just created.

2. Highlight the **User_Template** object and press **Enter**.

3. Highlight **View or edit properties of this object** and press **Enter.** A list of property categories is displayed. I'll show how to enter information in a few of these categories. You can enter information in the other categories in a similar manner.

Entering identification information

To enter identification information for the User_Template object, highlight **Identification** and press **Enter.** An Identification information screen is displayed that is similar to the one shown in Figure 12-3.

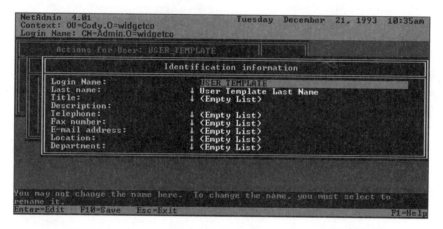

Figure 12-3. The Identification information screen in NETADMIN.

This screen lists the fixed information pertaining to user objects. However, some of the options available for users are not applicable for User_Templates. With the exception of Login Name (which cannot be changed from here), the values you enter in these fields are for information purposes only. The NetWare 4 operating system currently uses only the Login Name for processing.

Most of the fields in this screen display (Empty List), indicating the field can contain more than one item, but currently contains no entries. Any field that can contain multiple values also displays the down arrow (↓) to indicate the field may have more than one value. If there is at least one value, the first value in the list is displayed in the field. The down arrow is used as a notifier that there are additional values in the list. You must select the field to view the entire list.

For this example, assume your company has one main telephone number for everyone in the company, no matter where they are located. We'll enter the telephone number.

NOTE

This same procedure can be used for all of the lists displayed, not just for the telephone list.

1. Select **Telephone** from the list and press **Enter.** A blank *Telephone numbers* window is displayed.

2. Press **Ins** to add an item to the list.

3. Type the company telephone number and press **Enter.**

4. At this point you can do any of the following:

    • Press **Ins** to add another telephone number, such as a secondary number.

    • Press **Del** to delete a number from the list.

    • Press **Enter** to change a number in the list.

    • Press **Esc** to exit the list.

    • Press **F10** to save the list.

Since you are finished with the telephone number, save the list by pressing **F10.** Your company's telephone number has now been added to the User_Template.

5. Press **F10** a second time to save all of the Identification information.

Entering environment information

To enter default information about the network environment for the User_Template, highlight **Environment** in the list of options on the screen and press **Enter.** An Environment information screen similar to the one shown in Figure 12-4 is displayed.

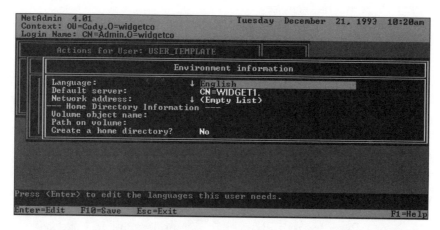

Figure 12-4. The Environment Information screen in NETADMIN.

Let's look at what information each of these fields contains or requires to supply valid information for new users.

The top three fields should already contain information.

- *Language.* The Language property specifies in which language the NetWare 4 utility screens should appear. The NetWare LOGIN program gets the value of the Language property and sets the DOS environment variable NWLANGUAGE to this value. In an English-speaking company, the NWLANGUAGE variable would be set to ENGLISH.

- *Default Server.* The NetWare SEND and BROADCAST utilities use the Default Server property to determine the server to which messages are sent. The SEND utility reads this property and sends the message to the user on this server. Any time you are logged in to the network, you should have an attachment to your Default Server so you can receive messages sent by others. If you are not logged in to your Default Server, or if you lose the connection, you won't be able to get any messages sent with the NetWare SEND or BROADCAST utilities.

- *Network Address.* The Network Address property lists the physical (or node) address from which the user is logged in. If the user is logged in from more than one workstation, the address of each of the workstation are displayed in this field. Note that only the first address in the list is automatically displayed. This property cannot be changed by the user or administrator; it is maintained by the server.

The Home Directory Information fields contain data necessary to create the user's home directory. Because NetWare 4 is not server centric, NETADMIN needs this information to determine where the user's home directory should be located. The fields under this heading include:

- *Volume object name.* This field contains the NDS name of the file system volume where the home directory will be created.

- *Path on volume.* This field specifies the file system directory path, beginning at the root of the specified volume, where you want to create the user's home directory.

- *Create a home directory?* prompt. The final screen prompt allows you to create the directory from this screen. This can be accomplished *only* if you have the proper file-system rights to create the user's home directory.

For our example, I'll set the Default Server and Home Directory information for this User_Template to allow you to create users in the chosen OU. By setting this information here, your user's home directories will be created properly. Leave the Language, Default Server, and Network Address fields as they currently are.

To accomplish these tasks, do the following:

1. Highlight **Volume object name** and press **Enter.**

2. Type in the name of the Volume on which you want to create the user's home directories. If you can't remember the volume's name, you can access the Browser at this point by pressing the **Ins** key.

3. Use the Browser to move to the context in which the server resides. When you find the right volume, highlight it and press **Enter.**

4. Press **Enter** again to accept the correct volume.

5. Now you need to set the correct path on the selected volume where you will create the home directories. You do not need to include the user's login name; this is added automatically when the user object is created. You also do not need to include the Server/Volume: portion, as the Volume object name already provides this information.

   If you know in which subdirectory you want to locate your users' home directories, it is easiest to simply type it in. (You can use the Browser instead if you so desire.) When the correct path appears, press **Enter.**

If the subdirectory already exists, the *Server/Volume:* field shows the correct information.

6. Answer **No** in the *Create a home directory?* field, since you don't want to create a home directory for the User_Template.

7. Press **F10** to save this information.

Entering default account restrictions

You might also want to set up some other default information before you go on to creating your users. This could include account restrictions such as the minimum password length and password expiration period. By putting this information into the User_Template, it can be automatically copied to all users created in this container.

The following steps can be used as an example of how to enter this information for the User_Template. You may want to set up your default account restrictions differently.

1. Highlight **Account Restrictions** and press **Enter.**

2. Highlight the **Password restrictions** field and press **Enter.**

3. Change **Require a password** to **Yes.**

4. Change **Force periodic password changes** to **Yes.**

5. Change **Days between forced changes** to the number of days you want between forced password changes.

6. Press **F10** to save this information.

You can add more information to the User_Template using the NETADMIN utility. The options we have shown introduce the basics of how to accomplish tasks using this utility. Remember, you can access context-sensitive help at any time in NETADMIN by pressing **F1.**

Creating User objects

Now that you've set up the User_Template object, I'll explain how to create actual User objects in the container. Remember, the administrator must have appropriate file-system rights prior to creating users if you plan to create home directories for them at the same time. Also make sure the administrator has all of the rights necessary to administer User and other NDS objects.

To create User objects in NETADMIN, complete the following steps:

1. Access the Browser screen.

2. Move to the proper context (the OU where you want to create the users).

3. Press **Insert** to add your first user object.

4. Select **User** from the *Select an object class* screen.

5. A screen with several empty fields is displayed. Enter information in the following fields:

   - Login Name: (the user's correct login name, such as GHERBON)

   - Last Name: (the user's last name, such as HERBON)

   - Create Home Directory: (Yes)

   - Copy the User_Template: (Yes)

   The user's Login Name can be more than eight characters long and can include characters that are not valid for DOS filenames. NetWare 4 includes a special routine that modifies the name entered in the Login Name field when creating home directories. However, to avoid confusion, we recommend that you remove any invalid characters and shorten the Login Name so it meets the DOS filename requirements.

Notice the Home Directory Information is already set for you. The path name is read from the Directory information that was saved in the User_Template object.

6. Press **F10** to create the user. A "wait" screen is displayed while the public and private encryption keys are generated.

Once this process is completed, you may want to exit NETADMIN and verify that the user's home directory was actually created and that it was created in the right place.

Repeat this process for every user you want to create in this context. Once you have created all of the users for this context, you can create a group.

Creating a Group object

A Group object assigns a name to a list of User objects that can be located anywhere in the Directory tree. A Group object is a handy shortcut for assigning rights to a group of users as a whole, rather than to individual users. The rights assigned to a Group object are granted to the individual users who belong to that group, no matter where the users are located in the Directory tree.

To create a group using NETADMIN, complete the following steps:

1. Using the Browser, move to the context of the container where you want to create the group. This can be either an O or an OU.

2. When you have selected the proper context, press **Ins.** This brings up the *Select an Object Class* screen.

3. Select **Group** and press **Enter.**

4. Type in the name for the group and information for any other fields on the active screen. Press **F10** to create the Group.

5. Once the group is created, select the group object to edit.

6. Select the **Group Members** option on the *View or Edit Group* screen. The screen initially displays (*Empty List*).

7. Press **Ins** twice. This returns you to the Browser screen and displays existing containers and users.

8. Use the Browser to move to the context in which you created your users.

9. Mark each user you want to be a member of the group by highlighting the user and pressing **F5**. Do not mark the User_Template object.

10. Press **Enter.** This adds all of the marked users to the group list.

11. You can add more users to the group list by pressing **Insert** twice and browsing for the other users to be added to the list. When you find the users you want to add to the list, mark each user as described in Step 9.

12. When you've added all of the users, press **F10** to save the list.

Adding these users to your group makes each user security equivalent to the group. Any rights you grant to the group are automatically granted to the members of the group.

Repeat this process for any other groups and users you want to be members of the groups.

Creating an Organizational Role object

An Organizational Role object defines a position, or "role," within an organization. An example of this might be a department manager who is assigned a specific set of duties or tasks. Any User object can be assigned to be an occupant of the Organizational Role object. An occupant of an Organizational Role object receives the same rights granted to the Organizational Role object.

To create an Organizational Role object in NETADMIN, complete the following steps:

1. Set your context to the container object where you want to create the Organizational Role.

2. Press **Insert.**

3. Select **Organizational Role** from the *Select an Object Class* list.

4. Type in a name for the Organizational Role and press **F10** to create the object.

Next you need to add a User object to the OR object's Role Membership property. Do this by completing the following steps:

1. Once the Organizational Role object has been created, select the OR from the Browser.

2. Select **View or edit properties of this object** and press **Enter.**

3. Select **Identification Information** and press **Enter.**

4. Select **Occupant** and press **Enter.**

5. Press **Insert** to add an occupant to this Organizational Role. An occupant of an Organizational Role is similar to being a member of a Group. Whenever a user is added as

an occupant of an Organizational Role, that user becomes security equivalent to the OR.

6. Browse for the user you want to add as an occupant of this role by pressing **Insert** until you find the correct User object. Select that User object and press **Enter** to add the user to the list.

To verify that the user object has been properly added to the Organizational Role, complete the following steps:

1. Return to the Browser.

2. Select the correct User object (the one you just added to the OR), and press **Enter.**

3. Select **View or Edit user** and press **Enter.**

   Check the screen fields to ensure that the following items are properly set:

   - *Require a password* is set to Yes.

   - *Force periodic password* is set to Yes.

   - *Days between forced changes* is set to the number you require.

   - *Telephone number* is correct.

   - *Security equal to* is set to the OR (the name of the Organizational Role should be shown in this field).

Creating a Directory Map object

The most frequent use of the Directory Map object is as a "pointer" to the path of a commonly used application, such as a spreadsheet or word processor. The Directory Map object makes it easier to upgrade to newer versions of your application without having to manually change everybody's drive mappings. When the application is upgraded, you can simply point the Directory Map to the new path of the software. Everyone having the Directory Map object in their login script automatically is able to access the new files.

To create a Directory Map object in NETADMIN, complete the following steps:

1. Set your context to the container where you want to create the Directory Map object.

2. Press **Insert.**

3. Select **Directory Map object** and press **Enter.** The *Create Object Directory Map* screen is displayed. On this screen are information fields for the following:

```
New name:
Volume object name:
Path on volume:
Name space type:
```

4. Fill in the *New name* field with the name of the application the Directory Map object points to (or whatever name you choose) and press **Enter.**

5. Fill in the *Volume object name* field with the volume where the application files reside and press **Enter.**

6. Set the path to the directory where the application files reside and press **Enter.**

For the user to be able to access the application directory in the Directory Map object, include the following line in the user's login script or in the container or profile of any of the users who need to access this program:

```
Map <drive>:= ".CN=<application name>
.OU=<OU name>.O=<O name>"
```

Substitute the correct context path for your particular Directory tree. Make sure you include the quotation marks as shown. Note that the user will need Read rights to the Directory Map object.

This maps your users to the application's directory. Whenever you upgrade to a newer version of your application, simply change the path in the Directory Map object to the application's new directory.

Assigning object rights (ACLs)

Another important task to understand is how to assign object rights using the NETADMIN utility. To give the local Admin all rights to his or her department's container, for example, you would complete the following steps:

1. Use the Browser to select the correct Organizational Unit.

2. Once the proper OU is selected, press **F10.**

3. Select **View or edit the trustees of this object** and press **Enter.**

4. In the *Trustees of this Object* screen, select **Trustees.** The Property, Rights, Trustee screen is displayed and shows the current trustee assignments.

5. Press the **Ins** key to create an ACL.

   Because you want to assign rights to the local administrator to allow him or her to be a manager of this container, give the local Admin all rights to the Access Control List (ACL) itself.

6. Highlight the Access Control List (ACL) property and press **Enter.** Enter the trustee name (the name of the local administrator) in this field and press **Enter.**

7. Select the object you want to become the trustee of this property by pressing **Ins.** The Browser screen is displayed.

8. Browse until you find the correct User object of your local administrator. Highlight the administrator's name and press **Enter.**

9. Press **Enter** again to accept the local administrator as the trustee. Note that the [R   ] (Read) right is given to this trustee by default.

10. To grant all rights to the trustee, press **Enter** on the Access Control List (ACL) line.

11. To see what rights are disallowed (not yet granted), press the **Ins** key again.

    The left side of the resulting screen shows which rights have been assigned to this trustee. The right side of the screen shows the rights not yet assigned to the trustee.

12. To assign all rights to the local administrator, use the **F5** key to mark all of the rights shown on the right side of the screen and press **Enter.**

13. After marking all of the rights, press **F10** to save the rights assignments. When this is done, you should see the local administrator's rights listed as [CRWAS] on the right side of the screen.

If you also want to make the local administrator a supervisor equivalent on the local server, you can assign the local administrator rights to the Server object. This allows the administrator access to the Server object and to the physical server itself. To accomplish this, you need to assign the local administrator the Supervisor privilege on the ACL property of the Server object.

To assign access privileges to a Server object, complete the following steps:

1. Select the correct Server object from the Browser and press **Enter.**

2. Select **View or edit the trustees of this object** and press **Enter.**

3. Select **Trustee** and press **Enter.**

4. At the next screen, press **Ins.**

5. Press **Ins** again to add a new trustee.

6. Select the ACL property and press **Enter.**

7. Select the local administrator and press **Enter.**

8. Mark the Supervisor right and press **F10.** The local administrator is now a supervisor equivalent on your local server. This show up on the *Property, Rights, Trustee* screen.

Adding and modifying other NDS objects is accomplished in a similar fashion.

Now that you are familiar with the NETADMIN utility, you should be able to use it to accomplish all of your NDS database management tasks. While the NetAdmin utility is not as "pretty" as the Windows-based NWAdmin utility, users already familiar with the C-Worthy interface in previous versions of NetWare may want to use it to accomplish their NDS administration tasks.

The next section discusses how to use NWAdmin to achieve some of the same things we've done using the NETADMIN utility.

Using the NWAdmin Utility

NetWare 4 includes a new Windows-based network administration utility known as NWAdmin. This utility is accessed by choosing the NetWare Administrator icon from the Windows Program Manager.

As shown in Figure 12-5, the NWAdmin administration utility shows the NDS tree in graphical form. The Browser portion of NWAdmin thus allows you to see the tree graphically as you use the mouse to move around the tree.

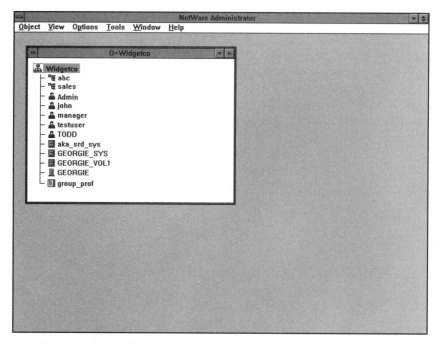

Figure 12-5. When you start NWAdmin, you see the Directory tree in graphical form.

As with the NetAdmin utility, you can press **F1** from anywhere in the NWAdmin utility to access context-sensitive help. This includes information on using the NWAdmin Browser as well as various other features.

Creating an NDS container object using NWAdmin

Again, before you can create leaf objects in the Directory tree, you must create the NDS container objects (Os and OUs). With this in mind, the following example creates a container in NWAdmin. As before, it also creates a User_Template object in each OU so you don't have to manually enter all information for the new User objects you add to the OU.

1. Start the NWAdmin utility by double-clicking on the NetWare Administrator icon in the Windows Program Manager.

2. Click on the container you want to hold the container object you are creating.

3. Select **Create** from the Object menu.

4. Highlight the new container object class in the New Object dialog box. Only objects that can be created in the current object appear in this list.

5. Click on the OK button to accept your selection. The Create object dialog box should display.

6. Type in the name of the new object in the box.

7. You have the option of defining additional properties. To do this, click on **Define Additional Properties** and enter the information for the additional properties you want to define.

8. You also have the option to Define User Defaults. This option lets you use the same default information in the new container as was in the parent container. This default information is stored in the USER_TEMPLATE object and is used every time you create a new user in this container.

9. When you are finished with the options in steps 7 and 8 (or if you skipped them), create the new container by choosing **Create.**

10. Once the new container is created, you are given the option of inheriting User_Template properties from the parent container. If you want to do this, choose **Yes.** If you want to define a new User_Template for the container, choose **No.**

11. If you chose **Yes** in Step 10, you are given the option of adding information to the object dialog box pages. If you don't want to add any information, go to Step 12.

12. Choose OK to save the properties you have just entered for your new container object.

Creating leaf objects in NWAdmin

Now that you've created a container object, you can create NDS leaf objects for such things as Users, Groups, Organizational Roles, Directory Maps, Printers, and so on. The administrator must have appropriate file system rights prior to creating users. Also make sure the administrator has all of the rights necessary to administer the user and other NDS objects (such as the Create object right to the container object that will contain the new leaf object).

To create leaf objects (such as a User object) in NWAdmin, complete the following steps:

1. Enter the NWAdmin utility by double-clicking on the NetWare Administrator icon in the Windows Program Manager.

2. Double-click on the container object that will contain the new leaf object.

3. Click on the **Create** option in the Object menu. The New Object dialog box is displayed.

4. Double-click on the class of object you want to create from the list in the New Object dialog box. Only those objects you can create in the current container appear in the list.

5. Click on OK to accept your object selection. A Create dialog box is displayed for the specified object you've chosen (see Figure 12-6). Each type of leaf object has a different Create dialog box. As always, you can click on the Help option for more specific information.

   Any fields displayed in the Create dialog box *must* be filled in with valid information.

   Any check boxes displayed in the Create dialog boxes are optional and do not require information. You usually check only one or the other of the optional check boxes. The available check boxes are:

   • Define Additional Properties

   • Create Another Object

   If you choose Define Additional Properties, an Identification dialog box is displayed next. If you choose Create Another Object, another Create dialog box is displayed.

6. When you are finished with the Create dialog box and its subordinate menus or dialog boxes, click on **Create** to create your new leaf object. You will either see an Identification dialog box or a Create Object dialog box, depending on the option you selected in Step 5.

7. Enter the required information for the dialog box that appears, and click on OK or **Create**. This saves all information and changes and returns you to the Browser screen.

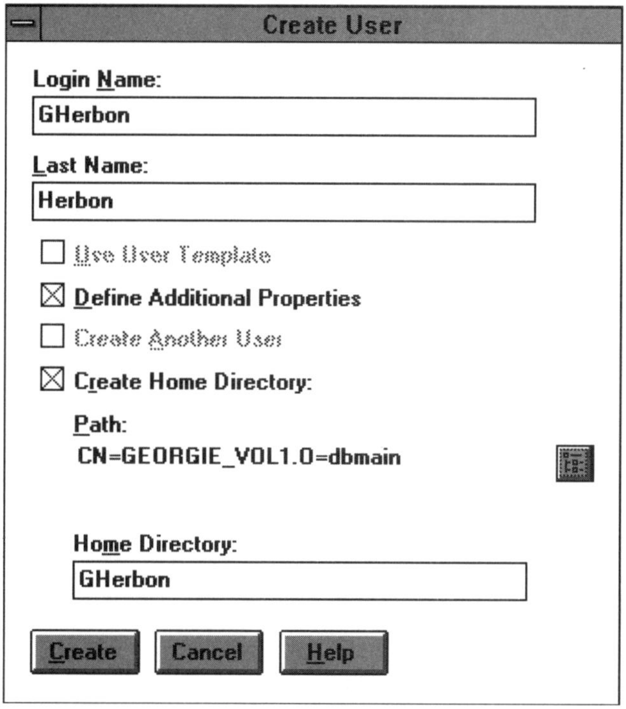

```
┌─────────────────────────────────────────────────┐
│ ▭                 Create User                     │
├─────────────────────────────────────────────────┤
│  Login Name:                                      │
│  ┌─────────────────────────────────────────────┐ │
│  │ GHerbon                                       │ │
│  └─────────────────────────────────────────────┘ │
│  Last Name:                                       │
│  ┌─────────────────────────────────────────────┐ │
│  │ Herbon                                        │ │
│  └─────────────────────────────────────────────┘ │
│                                                   │
│   ☐ Use User Template                             │
│   ☒ Define Additional Properties                  │
│   ☐ Create Another User                           │
│   ☒ Create Home Directory:                        │
│      Path:                                        │
│      CN=GEORGIE_VOL1.O=dbmain             ┌───┐   │
│                                           │   │   │
│                                           └───┘   │
│      Home Directory:                              │
│      ┌──────────────────────────────────────────┐│
│      │ GHerbon                                   ││
│      └──────────────────────────────────────────┘│
│                                                   │
│   ┌─────────┐  ┌─────────┐  ┌─────────┐           │
│   │ Create  │  │ Cancel  │  │  Help   │           │
│   └─────────┘  └─────────┘  └─────────┘           │
└─────────────────────────────────────────────────┘
```

Figure 12-6. The Create User dialog box.

With the NWAdmin utility, you create all other leaf objects in this same manner. As an example, I'll describe how to add members to a Group Object.

Adding members to a Group object

Group objects assign a name to a list of User objects that can be located anywhere in the Directory tree. You can then assign rights to the Group as a whole, rather than to individual users.

To add members to a group using NWAdmin, complete the following steps:

1. Using the NWAdmin Browser, select the group you want to add members to and double-click on it.

2. Click on the **Details** option in the Object menu.

3. Click on the **Members** button on the right side of the Object dialog box.

4. Click on the **Add** button to browse the Directory tree for the User Objects you want to add to the group.

5. Browse the Directory tree until the User object you want to add to the group is displayed in the Objects box.

6. Click on OK to accept this User object and add it to the group.

7. Click on the **Add** button again to add more User objects to the Group object. Repeat this step for every User object you want to add to the group.

8. When you are through adding User objects to the Group object, click on OK to save the information and return to the Browser screen.

Repeat this process for any other groups and users you want to be members of the groups.

Adding users to a group makes each user's security equivalent to the group. Any rights you grant to the group are automatically granted to the members of the group.

Other Features of the NetWare 4 Utilities

In addition to the various tasks listed in the preceding sections, the second release of NetWare 4 (version 4.01) added certain capabilities to make Directory management easier. These added features allow the administrator to do the following:

- Rename a leaf object without deleting and recreating the object.

- Move a leaf object to any other container that resides in the same Directory tree. This is done through a mark and drag process in NWAdmin.

- Move all of the objects that reside in one container to another container. This is done by using NWAdmin to create a new container. You can then mark all of the objects you want to move and use the mouse to drag all of the objects to the new container. This feature allows you to move or rename an OU (such as a department) and all of the objects in that department.

Future updates of the NetWare 4 utilities are expected to include features that allow the administrator to do the following:

- *Rename a container*. This feature allows the administrator to change the name of a container object when departments or divisions change names.

- *Move a subtree.* This feature allows the administrator to move a complete branch (or subtree) of the Directory tree in one single operation. You will be able to select an entire container (and all objects in the container) and move it to a different part of the Directory tree.

- *Merge trees.* This feature allows the administrator to merge two completely different Directory trees into one tree.

Once these new features are incorporated into NetWare 4, you can more easily plan and implement smaller divisional or departmental trees, and later merge those trees together to form an enterprise-wide or global Directory tree. This would allow more flexibility in restructuring the Directory tree, in case things don't work perfectly in the initial Directory implementation. It will also better accommodate companies that are constantly changing or growing.

Summary

The NetWare 4 administration utilities are flexible and can be used for more tasks than are listed here. This chapter has shown some basics for using both the NETADMIN utility and the NWAdmin utility. From these examples, you should be able to accomplish all of your NDS database management tasks. Remember, the utilities provide quick help information as well as context-sensitive help. The easiest way to learn what you can and can't do with these utilities is to use them.

If you need specific step-by-step information on using these utilities, refer to the NetWare 4 documentation set. For a good tutorial on the NETADMIN text-based utility, see the July 1993 issue of *NetWare Application Notes*.

Managing Partitions and Replicas

This chapter discusses the information you need to consider when managing the partitioning and replication of your Directory tree. In NetWare Directory Services, partition management (the creation, replication, and distribution of NDS partitions) is an important part of making your network as efficient, easy to use, and fault tolerant as possible. If you have followed the recommendations in Chapter 4 and planned your partition replication and distribution scheme ahead of time, you should be able to manage partitions and replicas easily and effectively.

The main ideas we want to cover in this chapter are when and why you need to manage partitions and replicas. I'll first review some partition management concepts, and then talk about some situations in which you might need to modify your partitions and replicas. At the end of the chapter are instructions for creating a new partition using the PARTMGR text-based utility and using the Partition Manager option in the NWAdmin graphical utility. For step-by-step instructions for completing all other partition management tasks, refer to your NetWare 4 documentation.

Partition Management Concepts

Partition management is an important part of having an efficient Directory tree that is easy to access. Partition management includes such tasks as:

- Creating a new partition

- Splitting a large partition into several smaller ones

- Joining or merging a partition with its parent partition

- Repairing damaged partitions

- Adding new replicas

- Deleting existing replicas

Most of these functions are major network operations. As such, they should not be considered tasks that someone can do in their spare time. Operations such as creating a new partition and merging an existing partition with a parent partition should be scheduled events on the network. Both of these operations make several changes to the network and temporarily affect Directory synchronization.

Be patient when performing these operations. The time it takes to successfully complete these operations depends on the size of the partitions and the number of replicas distributed around the network. Planning ahead and scheduling time for partition management functions will pay dividends in network performance and ease of access for your users.

Pointers and replica rings

A brief discussion of how partitions use pointers and what replica rings are will help you better understand how NDS partitioning works. To find information in the Directory tree, NDS uses a process called *tree-walking*, in which searches are performed up and down the tree until the proper information is returned. Inter-partition searches are accomplished through the use of pointers. Every Directory partition stores a pointer to the partition that is immediately superior to it, as well as a pointer to any partitions that are subordinate to it. NDS uses these pointers to find requested information that does not reside on the immediate partition.

Replica pointers include the following information:

- The name of the server on which the replica is located

- The address of the server the replica resides on

- The type and current state of the replica

- The replica number

A replica ring includes all of the replica pointers of a partition. This ring is used to provide direct update information to the proper replicas in an efficient manner. The ring can be considered a mini-database of information specific to a certain partition and all of the replicas of that partition.

Each partition in a Directory tree has its own specific set of information. Again, this information is stored and used only for the replicas that are part of the ring—those that belong to the same partition.

Placement of partitions

When you set up Directory partitions, you should do it in a way that makes sense to you and your users. You can also use partitions to group together users that access the same resources. For instance, accounting departments usually have separate accounts payable and accounts receivable groups. Both groups need to access the same software and resources (such as applications and printers). They also need to share data on a regular basis. In this case, it makes sense to place both of these groups in the same Directory partition. They can easily access the network resources they need, without having to search different sections of the Directory tree to find and access these resources.

If you have a geographically dispersed network, consider where the different parts of your Directory tree will be located, and what parts of the tree will be accessed from other locations (over a WAN link) on a regular basis. Partitions should be created as close to leaf objects as is practical. In other words, avoid having numerous levels of container objects included in the same partition as much as possible.

Size of partitions

Generally, you should try to keep your partitions small, since smaller partitions require shorter times to update or synchronize. We recommend that you try to limit your partitions to under 1,000 objects each. However, try not to have a partition that contains less than 100 NDS objects.

T I P

It is difficult to determine the exact impact the size of partition will have on the network. However, you can get a rough estimate by determining the number of objects in the partition and then figuring how often changes are made to objects in that partition. For instance, if a User object averages two changes per hour, you can estimate an approximate number of changes by multiplying the number of users in a partition by the average number of changes in a given time. For 200 users at two changes per hour, the result would be 400 changes per hour. Note that this varies according to the type of NDS objects in the partition. User objects usually undergo more modifications than printer or server objects.

Purposes of partitioning and replication

As explained in Chapter 4, there are two main purposes for replicating partitions in NetWare 4. The first one is to provide faster access to Directory information. If you use WAN links for constantly accessing network resources, it is often helpful to create a local replica of the partition that contains the most frequently used information. That way, the remote site does not have to send a constant stream of packets across the WAN link just to access NDS information. This "local" access to distant information results in better network performance (fewer packets across WAN links) and quicker local access to the necessary information.

The second purpose for creating replicas of your partitions is provide Directory fault tolerance. (Remember, Directory fault tolerance is different from system fault tolerance. For more information on system fault tolerance, refer to the NetWare 4 documentation.) Having more than one copy of a partition protects the information stored in that partition from being lost in the event of server failures.

Multiple replicas also permit users to login to the network and access those servers and resources that are currently active, even if their default (or home) server is off-line at the time. Having replicas of the different partitions distributed around the network provides redundant NDS tree information (including client login information). Any server that holds a replica of the necessary partition can provide the information a user needs to login and access the network. Of course, the user won't be able to access applications or data that reside on the inoperational server until it is brought back up again.

To provide the best possible Directory fault tolerance, be sure you have an adequate number of copies of each partition and these replicas are efficiently placed around the network. I recommend you have no fewer than five copies of each partition stored on your network.

However, don't get carried away with replication. I recommend you keep no more than eight replicas on any production server. Having more than eight replicas may decrease the server's performance during NDS synchronization. While in most cases the slowdown is negligible, you may get some user complaints about the server being slow.

Many people have questions about which backup product they should use to back up NDS information. Currently, the best backup for NDS is to have several copies of your replicas (preferably read/write copies) spread around the network. A damaged or lost replica can then be rebuilt or copied from an existing replica.

Large NetWare 4 sites have been known to maintain certain servers that contain nothing but replicas. This practice ensures a backup copy of each partition is readily available. (The replica copies on these servers can be used for both backup and fault tolerance purposes. You do not need multiple copies of the same replica on these servers.) To protect NDS information against a major disaster, you should also consider maintaining an off-site server that holds copies of all of your replicas.

Assessing the Effectiveness of Your Partitions and Replicas

To determine how well your partitioning and replication is working, it is a good idea to draw a map of your Directory tree so you can see how the information flows around your network. This makes it easier to pinpoint effective ways to provide easy access of NDS information to your clients, and to provide Directory fault tolerance. Every time you add to your Directory tree, consider the implications of information flow and fault tolerance, and add or distribute new replicas accordingly.

As your Directory tree grows or changes, there may be times when you will want to split partitions apart. This might be the case if a partition grows too big to easily manage or takes a long time to synchronize.

On the other hand, there may be times when you will want to merge partitions together to provide for easier access or management, as in Figure 13-2. For example, if you move a number of objects out of a particular container, its partition may become too small to justify being a separate partition anymore. Joining it with its parent partition means one less partition to worry about.

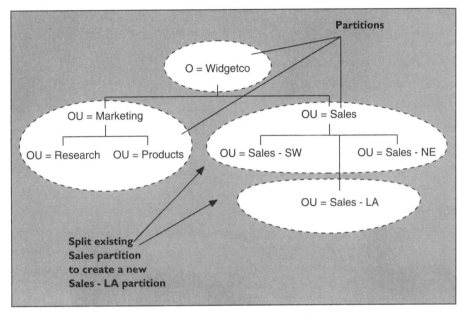

Figure 13-1. Splitting a partition that has become too big.

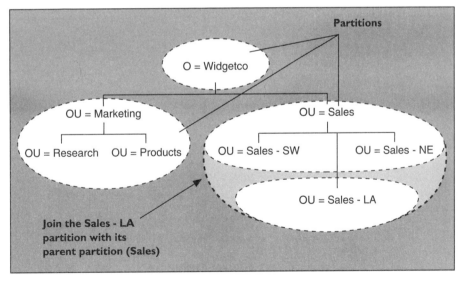

Figure 13-2. Joining two partitions together to simplify administration.

Never try to split or join a partition that is experiencing problems. Attempting to do this will compound the problem rather than eliminate it. Split or join only stable partitions that have not been problematic, or repair the problem partition before attempting these operations. Refer to Chapter 14 for ways to resolve partition problems.

Steps for Replicating a Partition

Partition management tasks can be performed using either the NetWare 4 PARTMGR text-based utility or by using the Partition Manager menu option in the NWAdmin GUI utility. The following examples illustrate how to replicate a partition with each utility. For instructions on how to perform other tasks, refer to your NetWare 4 documentation.

Using the PARTMGR utility

Following are the steps necessary to replicate a Directory partition using the PARTMGR utility:

1. To access the utility, type **PARTMGR** and press **Enter.**

2. Select the context (partition) you want to replicate, and press **F10** to choose the management options for the selected partition.

3. In the Partition Management screen, select the **View/Edit Replicas** option and press **Enter.**

4. The Replicas stored on server screen is displayed. Add a replica of the selected partition by pressing **Ins.**

5. The Add replica screen is displayed, as shown in Figure 13-3.

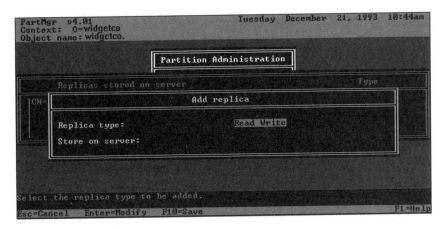

Figure 13-3. The Add replica screen in PARTMGR.

In the *Replica type* field, enter the type (Read Write or Read Only) for the new replica. In the *Store on server* field, enter the name of the server on which you want to store the new replica.

6. Press **F10** to save the information.

7. You can create another replica by repeating steps 1 through 6. Or, you can exit the utility by pressing **Esc** continuously until you reach the exit prompt. Answer **Yes** to the exit prompt and press **Enter** to confirm your choice.

You can accomplish all of your partition and replica management tasks using the text-based PARTMGR utility. This utility's interface should feel familiar to anyone who has administered previous versions of NetWare. For experienced NetWare users, the PARTMGR utility may be the easiest way to manage partitions and replicas.

257

Using NWAdmin's Partition Manager tool

For those who are new to NetWare, the Partition Manager option provided in the Tools menu of the NWAdmin graphical utility may be easier to use. The NWAdmin utility provides Directory tree information in graphical form and it allows for point-and-click functions. This section gives an example of using the Partition Manager function in the NWAdmin utility.

To create a replica by using the Partition Manager option in the NWAdmin Tools menu, complete the following steps:

1. Start the NWAdmin utility by double-clicking on the NetWare Administrator icon in the Windows Program Manager.

2. Highlight and click on the **Partition Manager** option in the Tools menu.

3. Use the Browser to browse through the Partitions screen to find the NDS container object for which you want to create a partition. If the container object doesn't appear in the window, you can browse the tree by selecting one of the objects that does appear, and then looking at that object's subordinates. Choosing **Help** provides more specific information on using this utility.

4. When you've found the correct container object, highlight it and choose **Create as new partition**. See Figure 13-4.

   This creates the desired partition and places a Master replica on the same server that holds the parent partition's Master replica.

5. To make sure the partition was created and to find out where the Master replica is stored, highlight the Organization or Organizational Unit you just created and

choose **Replicas.** This brings up a screen that shows you the name of the server on which the partition is stored, and the partition type.

At this point you are finished creating a new partition. You can create more partitions by repeating steps 1 through 5 above, or you can move on to various other NDS administrative tasks.

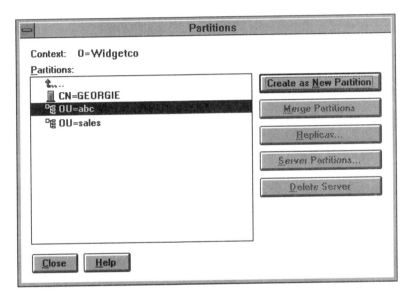

Figure 13-4. Creating a new partition in NWAdmin.

Summary

This chapter has provided an overview of what partition and replica management is and the things you need to consider before creating or modifying your Directory partitions and replicas. With this information, you should be able to efficiently manage and use partitions and replicas to make your Directory as efficient, reliable, and user-friendly as possible.

259

Troubleshooting Common NDS Problems

A number of new and interesting things can sometimes occur when installing and implementing NetWare Directory Services. Bear in mind that many of what people term "problems" with NDS are things that can be avoided if you carefully plan and implement the Directory tree according to the guidelines in this book. This chapter looks at some of the most common problems that have been encountered with NDS and gives suggestions for resolving them.

Tips for Avoiding Common NDS Problems

Following a few simple rules can help you avoid most problems when using NDS. Use these rules as guidelines for using Directory Services:

- Remember that "pilot errors" (those caused by user mistakes) are much more frequent than problems in the software itself. Do not immediately assume that NDS is at fault.

- Whenever you are entering the name of an object or service, be sure to type the proper name with the correct spelling. This is necessary during object creation as well as during searches and when accessing resources. Misspelling or mistyping names has caused more problems than you would believe.

- Be sure to use the proper spelling and syntax when searching for properties of NDS objects.

- Be familiar with established naming conventions for objects and properties. Follow the rules and limitations for container and leaf object names outlined in Appendix A.

- Remember that Directory Services is different from the NetWare file system directories. When people assume the two are the same, various unnecessary problems can arise.

- When looking for a partition, be sure you know the exact name of the partition and that the partition you're looking for actually exists.

- Make sure all NDS objects in the same container have unique names. NDS will not allow you to create a new object with the same name as an existing object. Pay attention to the screen prompts whenever using the NetWare 4 utilities to manipulate objects.

- Never try to put more than one copy of the same replica on a server.

- If an NDS operation fails, wait a few minutes and retry the operation. Don't immediately jump to the conclusion that there is a serious problem.

- If you get "access denied" messages, check the easy things first before assuming there is a serious problem with NDS. It might be something as simple as a user not having sufficient rights to an object or service on the network.

Undoubtedly, people will find innovative ways to use NDS that result in situations that have never been encountered before. Stepping back and considering the problem often helps more than knee-jerk reactions. Use proper troubleshooting techniques to identify, isolate, and resolve problems. It is also a good idea to keep a log of problems and what you did to resolve them.

The remainder of this chapter contains suggestions for resolving specific problems in NetWare 4.

Installation Failure

For security or other reasons, many sites set up their Directory tree to allow for central administration of the upper levels of the tree, and distributed (local) administration of the lower levels. In this type of setup, administrators at the lower portions of the tree may encounter a problem when installing the first server into a new Organizational Unit.

The NetWare 4 INSTALL NLM automatically creates a new Directory partition when a server is installed in a new container. An attempt is also made to replicate this partition in the parent partition. The problem arises when the administrator at the lower level of the tree does not have the necessary rights to create an NDS partition in the parent level. This causes the installation process to fail during the Directory Services portion of the program.

To prevent this scenario from happening, do the following prior to installing the first server in the container:

1. Run NETADMIN or NWAdmin and create the new OU container in its proper location in the Directory tree.

2. Start one of the NetWare 4 Partition Management utilities—PARTMGR or the Partition Manager option in NWAdmin.

3. Select the partition you just created and choose the **Modify Partitions** option. When you are asked if you want to create a new partition, answer **Yes.** The utility creates a new partition and automatically stores a master replica of that partition on the server that resides in the parent partition and is closest to the Directory root. It also places read/write replicas on every server that stores replicas of the new partition's parent partition.

Now, when the User object assigned to manage the new partition installs the first server into that container, a screen prompt in the INSTALL program asks, Do you want to create a partition replica on the new server? The administrator should answer **Yes** to this question. A read/write replica of the new partition is placed on the new server, and the installation will succeed.

Once the new server is installed, you can use either of the partition management utilities to change the read/write replica on your new server to a master replica.

Any time you make a change to the Directory (such as replicating a partition or adding a new server to the tree), you need to allow the network time to synchronize before making further changes. For example, if you add a new server to the Directory, be sure to allow at least 30 minutes (longer if synchronization is occurring over a WAN link) before attempting to replicate the partition that contains the new server.

Accidental Deletion of the Administrative User

In NetWare 4, the Admin object is a regular User object just like any other User object. It can be deleted, and its rights can be restricted at various levels of the tree. This gives you the flexibility to create as many administrative User objects as needed to properly administer the Directory. When doing this, you should carefully follow the recommendations given earlier in this book to ensure you have all branches of the tree covered. Also take care to document the correct names and passwords for all administrative User objects created in the tree.

If you accidentally delete an administrative user without having created a backup user who has explicit rights of the Admin user at the root, you will lose the ability to manage that portion of the tree. Forgetting or losing the Admin's password is another potential problem that could have the same result.

Avoid having only one person who knows the password. If that person suddenly becomes ill or leaves the company, you'll need some way of knowing what the password was. Always have a contingency plan in place to guard against this eventuality.

If you do lose control of all or part of the tree (either by deleting Admin or losing a password), there is a way to regain control. *Do not* try to reinstall Directory Services all over again. This will not solve the problem! Instead, call Novell Technical Support at 1-800-NETWARE. They have a workaround for overcoming this obstacle. You will have to pay for the fix, but the resolution of the problem should be immediate.

N O T E This is a one-time fix. If you should happen to commit the same error in another part of the Directory tree or at a later time, you will have to call Novell Tech Support again. The original solution only works once.

NDS Synchronization

The most common NDS error messages are generated because the Directory is loosely consistent and simply has not had time to properly update all of the replicas in a replica ring. Most of the time, all you need to do is wait a few minutes and retry the operation. Give this a try before considering more drastic measures.

Waiting for Directory synchronization

Directory synchronization is the process of updating or synchronizing information to all copies of a partition that reside on the network. Synchronization is an automatic background process that requires no user intervention.

During synchronization, any new information (updates) stored in the partition are sent to all replicas of that partition, along with a time stamp telling when the update was received. Time stamps ensure that only the newest information will be updated, since information with a later time stamp always takes precedence over older information.

Note that only the delta changes—those changes made since the last synchronization pass took place—are propagated. These are determined by the In Sync Up To information kept by each replica. Each server receives each change only once. Every time the replica is updated, the In Sync Up To attributes are updated as well.

There is no set time to wait for synchronization to complete in between major Directory operations. As a general guideline, wait about 30 minutes if your network is located in a single location and has 30 servers or fewer. If you have server connected over WAN links, you may have to wait several hours if the partition is replicated over the WAN links. While the synchronization process does take some time, it enables the Directory to provide consistent information across the entire network.

Directory Out of Sync

NetWare Directory Services is a "loosely consistent" database. At any given point in time, the whole Directory may not be in perfect synchronization, but "most" of the Directory will be in sync. NDS was designed this way so as to allow Directory information to be distributed without burdening the network with unnecessary synchronization traffic.

If you do see a message stating that the Directory is out of sync, there are several things you should do:

- Determine whether more than one client is getting this error. Since the Directory is loosely consistent, there are times when it may be out of sync for a short time. If you suspect this to be the case (as it often is when many clients get the same error message), just wait a while. The Directory should return to a synchronized state.

- If only one client receives the error, check the parameter settings in its NET.CFG file. See Chapter 10 for more information about NET.CFG file settings.

267

If the problem remains unresolved, you may need to run the DSREPAIR utility as instructed in the NetWare 4 documentation. DSREPAIR runs on a single server and corrects inconsistent data on the replicas of that server only. It is not a global repair. A log of the repair process is kept in the DSREPAIR.LOG file in the SYS:SYSTEM directory of the server.

In the course of running DSREPAIR, it may become necessary to rebuild one or more replicas, remove and then recreate replicas, or resynchronize one or more of the replica rings on your network. This can be a time-consuming process, so be patient. Any resulting replica repair is better than just living with the problem.

 Never try to split or join a partition that is experiencing problems. Attempting to do this will compound the problem rather than eliminate it. Run DSREPAIR first to resolve the problem with the partition.

Unknown objects in the Directory

Occasionally you might run across an "unknown" object in the Directory tree. These unknown objects are usually nothing to worry about. They are created as placeholders during certain Directory replication operations, and usually appear after you restore a replica or run the DSREPAIR utility. NDS labels an object as unknown to indicate that the object is still intact, but is missing a mandatory property for the class the object belongs to. You can delete unknown objects using the NETADMIN or NWAdmin utilities.

Time Synchronization Problems

When time fails to synchronize on the network, the most likely reason is that there are no reachable time sources. Check your time-synchronization configuration to be sure it is correctly set up and that time sources are running and synchronized. Remember, a secondary time server will not synchronize until its time source is synchronized.

Time synchronization uses NetWare's routing functions. Keep in mind that it may take a while for routing information to reach a particular time source. Wait a few minutes before you jump to conclusions about why a server won't synchronize its time. Also, use the DISPLAY SERVERS command at the server console to see if the target server can be seen from the server in question.

Always set the DOS time *before* booting a NetWare 4 server to make sure the hardware clock has the correct time. *Never* set the time backwards!

Also, be careful whenever you change local time information. If you misconfigure local time while time synchronization is active, NetWare will attempt to adjust UTC time to correspond to network time (which, in turn, controls local time). Thus the time synchronization feature can actually fight your efforts to correct misconfigured local time. The proper way to reconfigure local time is to unload TIMESYNC.NLM, set the local time correctly, and then reload the NLM.

NOTE   In NetWare 4.01, TIMESYNC.NLM is not shipped as a separate module. If you unload TIMESYNC, you won't be able to load it again. To get a copy of the NLM as a separate module, contact Novell Technical Support at 1-800-NETWARE.

Time Not Synchronized error

You may receive an error that time is not synchronized (error 659 or FD6D hex). Yet when you check the server's status with the TIME command, it reports that time is synchronized. This error actually means that NDS has received a time stamp that is older than information already in the Directory database. The probable cause is that the server time has been set backwards, which could result from a dead CMOS battery or the time being set wrong when the server was booted.

Debug parameters

Time synchronization has several undocumented parameters that were implemented for debugging, testing, and fine tuning of the synchronization algorithm. They aren't documented because they may be changed or eliminated in future releases. However, they can be useful in troubleshooting time synchronization problems.

The first parameter activates the display of time sync debug information on the server console screen. To enable this feature, type **SET TIMESYNC Debug=7** and press **Enter.**

Various messages are displayed that reflect time synchronization activity on that server, including which servers are being polled and what time adjustments are being made. To turn off this display, type: **SET TIME-SYNC Debug=0** and press **Enter.**

Another undocumented parameter is the following SET command:

SET TIMESYNC Immediate Synchronization=On

This command awakens the synchronization process and causes it to start a polling loop. Type this command after setting the debug flag to cause some screen output immediately, rather than waiting for the process to awaken normally.

Working with NetWare 4 Servers in the Tree

In NDS, NetWare Server objects must be treated somewhat carefully. This section gives some pointers for working with NetWare 4 Servers.

Renaming a NetWare 4 server

When you need to rename a NetWare 4 server or change its internal net number, *do not* use the NetWare administrative utilities (NETADMIN or NWAdmin). For NDS to recognize and include the server in the Directory, you must manually change these server values in the server's AUTOEXEC.NCF file. Once the changes are made, bring down the server and reboot it.

With NDS, each NetWare 4 server manages its own Server object in the tree. When the server comes back online, NDS will recognize the change and update the Server object with the newly specified information. The new information is then propagated to all necessary replicas of the server's partition as part of the synchronization process.

Be aware that changing server names and internal net numbers is a major operation because of the resynchronization that is involved. It should only be done with forethought and only when absolutely necessary.

Moving a Server in the Directory tree

The operation of moving a Server object to a different location in the tree is much simpler than renaming a server. To relocate a Server object, simply use the Move option in either of the NetWare 4 administrative utilities (NETADMIN or NWAdmin).

Removing Server objects from the tree

If you need to remove an operational server from the tree temporarily, proceed as follows:

1. Using the partition management utilities (NWAdmin or PARTMGR), move all master replicas stored on the server to other servers. Then remove all replicas from the server.

2. Allow at least 15 minutes for the Directory to synchronize.

3. Using either NWAdmin or NETADMIN, delete the Server object.

To remove a failed or disconnected server, do the following:

1. If a master replica was stored on the failed server, use DSREPAIR to designate a new master elsewhere.

2. Using either NWAdmin or NETADMIN, delete the Server object.

Viewing server configuration information

NetWare 4 has a useful command to dump configuration information to a file: At the server console, type **LOAD REGISTER C** and press **Enter.**

This creates a text file called CONFIG.NFO in the SYS:SYSTEM directory of the server. The file's contents will be similar to the following:

```
Server Name:  WIDGETC01
OS version: 4.1
OS revision number: 0
 Novell NetWare v4.01  July 12, 1993
Serial Number: 00001384
Licensed Connections: 100
Internal Network Address: 0030A35F
Security Restriction Level: 1
SFT Level: 2
TTS Level: 1
Server memory: 14,547,968 bytes
Cache buffer size: 4096
Original cache buffers: 2175
Directory cache buffers: 22
Sectors per cache buffer: 8
Server type: Normal Server
Server language: ENGLISH (4)
```

```
Processor Speed Rating: 152
LAN card configuration
NE2 [slot=1 frame=ETHERNET_802.2]
 Version 3.21
 Node Address: 00001B048722
 Protocols:
  IPX
    Network Address: 01030551
Disk Drive Configuration
Device # 0 PS/2 ESDI (0F000004)
PS/2 ESDI  Card 0 Controller 4 Drive 0
Volume Segments on Drive:
 102 Megabytes on Volume SYS segment 0
 Read After Write Verify: Software Level
 Drive Operating Status: Active
 . . .
```

The DSTRACE Option

This is an undocumented feature in NetWare 4 that displays messages about what NDS is doing on the server console screen. To activate this feature, type **SET DSTRACE=ON** at the server console. Other functions are available:

- SET DSTRACE=DEBUG turns on the display of debugging information. Don't leave this option on indefinitely. It can affect the server's ability to perform other diagnostic functions.

- SET DSTRACE=NODEBUG turns off the display of debugging information.

273

- SET TTF=ON starts writing DSTRACE information to a file called DSTRACE.DBG in the SYS:SYSTEM directory of the server.

- SET TTF=OFF stops the writing of DSTRACE information to the DSTRACE.DBG file.

- SET DSTRACE=OFF turns off the DSTRACE function.

NDS and TTS

Activate NetWare's Transaction Tracking System (TTS) on all Directory Services servers and check periodically to see that TTS is still enabled. When TTS is disabled on an NDS server, any Directory operations that require modifications to the NDS database are also disabled.

When booting the server, always back out TTS transactions. Failure to back out partial transactions may cause the NDS database to be damaged. You can set up the server to automatically back out TTS transactions by placing the following statement in the STARTUP.NCF file:

```
SET Auto TTS Backout Flag=ON
```

Troubleshooting NDS Rights

With the extra levels of object and property rights, it may be harder to troubleshoot NDS rights assignments. Following are some guidelines to help you figure out what may be wrong. If a User object seems to have too many rights, check these items:

- Explicit trustee assignments for:

  - the User object itself.

  - any Groups the user is a member of.

- any Organizational Role the user is an occupant of.

- security equivalences the user may have.

- rights assigned to containers the user is in (up the tree to the [Root]).

- Inherited rights from any explicit trustee assignments further up the tree.

- Trustee assignments made at the container level—check Trustees of this Object in NETADMIN or NWAdmin.

- Whether the user is in a container or group, or is security equivalent to something, that has rights to the container.

If a user is not receiving rights you think he or she should have in a container, check the following:

- If you expect the user to receive rights from being in a container, check the rights assigned at the container level.

- If you expect the user to receive rights by virtue of a security equivalence or by membership in a group or organizational role, check the rights assigned to those items. Also check to make sure the user is indeed a member of the group or an occupant of the organizational role.

- There may be an Inherited Rights Filter at a higher container level that is blocking rights. Check the parent containers for IRFs and make explicit assignments if necessary.

Backing Up NetWare 4 Information

Currently, the best way to back up the NDS database is through adequate replication.

To back up the NetWare 4 file system data and trustee information, you can also use backup products that work with NetWare 2 and 3. Remember, however, that there are no bindery files to back up on a NetWare 4 server. Also, these products can only backup and restore file system trustees for objects in the bindery emulation context. To back up both NDS and the NetWare 4 file system use a system written to Novell's Storage Management Services (SMS) specification. Many third-party vendors are updating their backup products to work with NetWare 4 and SMS. Check with your vendor to see if a revision is in the works.

Make sure the backup program backs up trustees by name rather than by ID number. If your backup software goes by ID numbers and you "lose" a disk that holds the Directory information for that server as well as the trustee rights, you will not be able to restore the trustee rights. Backing up by name ensures that if you ever need to restore this information, you won't lose the trustee rights and be forced to reinstate all the trustee rights manually.

Summary

As with most any sophisticated software, you will find the greatest success with NetWare 4 and Directory Services if you take the time to read the available instructions and follow them carefully. By consulting this book and other sources of information available (see the listing in Appendix B), you should be able to avoid most potential problems with NDS.

As you gain experience with resolving NDS problems, or whenever you encounter some interesting aspect of planning or implementing NetWare 4 Directory Services, consider sharing what you have learned with others. A good place to do this is on Novell's NetWire forums on CompuServe. Knowledgeable users and engineers monitor these forums and can help you share any ideas and helpful information you might have.

Section 4

Appendices, Glossary & Index

NDS Object Naming

This appendix discusses NDS object naming and provides an example of an NDS naming standards document. This information is meant only as a guideline to give you some insights on how to set up your own NDS naming standards. Your document can be as simple as that shown here, or as complex as you need to make it. The complexity is limited only by the physical restrictions of the NDS property fields.

The examples in this appendix will help you create your own naming standards for NetWare Directory Services. Remember, these samples are meant to assist network supervisors in implementing object names and property values in a consistent manner throughout the Directory tree.

Figures A-1 through A-4 provide examples of naming standards that can be used for NDS User objects. Figure A-5 shows examples for naming Organization container objects. Following these tables is a section that provides suggestions for naming your network resources to make access easier for your users.

PROPERTY	SUGGESTED FORMAT	EXAMPLE
Login name	First initial and last name of user. Capitalize all letters in the login name. Be sure this name is unique.	LHERBON
Full name	User's surname, followed by a comma, followed by the first name and middle initial. Capitalize only the first letter in each name.	Herbon, Leann A.
Other names	No set standard. You can decide on your own usage.	
Title	User's current job title.	Vice President
Description	No set standard. You can decide on your own usage.	
Telephone	Full telephone number.	800-555-1212
FAX number	Full fax number.	800-555-1313
EMAIL address	E-mail address.	LHERBON @WIDGETCO
Location	Name or code for building where user is located.	BLDG 7
Department	Department code (for accounting or other system).	01-452

Figure A-1. Identification properties for NDS User objects.

PROPERTY	SUGGESTED FORMAT
Login restrictions	Set according to your company's security practices. By default, all of the fields in this property are set to No.
Password restrictions	Set according to your company's security practices. Recommended settings are discussed in the security section of the NetWare 4 documentation.
Time restrictions	No standard. Choose your own.
Net address restrictions	No standard. Choose your own.
Intruder lockout status	No standard. Choose your own.
Account balance	No standard. Choose your own.
Volume	No standard. Choose your own.

Figure A-2. Account restriction properties for NDS User objects.

PROPERTY	SUGGESTED FORMAT	EXAMPLE
Language	User's primary language.	ENGLISH (US)
Default server	Server the user receives messages on when sent with the SEND utility.	SALES_SW
Network address	No set standard. You should devise your own network address standards.	
Home directory	Include both the Volume object name and the path name.	WC-SYS:\HOME\LHERBON

Figure A-3. Environment properties for NDS User objects.

PROPERTY	SUGGESTED FORMAT
Postal address	User's default corporate postal address. Place the mail stop information in the Post Office Box field. Example: 123 TECHNOLOGY STREET TECHVILLE, USA 12345 Use **Copy the address to the mailing label** to set the mailing address. Use the full name on the mailing label.

Figure A-4. Example of postal address properties for NDS User objects.

PROPERTY	SUGGESTED FORMAT	EXAMPLE
Name	Full name of the organization associated with this container.	Widgetco
Other name	No standard. Choose your own.	
Description	Brief description of the organization's job functions.	Design, production, and sales of widgets, gidgets, and gizmos
Telephone	Full telephone number as used in the company's telephone directory.	800-555-4567
FAX number	Full fax number as used in the company's telephone directory.	800-555-7654
Location	Current location names found in the company's telephone directory. If the organization is located in different geographical areas, put all locations in the field.	Washington D.C., Cody, Phoenix

Figure A-5. Properties for Organization container objects.

Guidelines for Naming NDS Container and Leaf Objects

Observe the following rules and limitations when naming NDS container and leaf objects.

General guidelines

The most effective object names are those that are short and easily identifiable.

- Although object names can be up to 64 characters in length, shorter is usually better. Users can remember short names more easily.

- Container object names should be intuitive and readily identify a part of the company, a project team, or similar division in the organization. Users will thus be able to remember their Directory contexts more easily and change contexts more quickly.

- Leaf object names should also be as descriptive as possible so users can easily remember them and search for the leaf objects they need to access. (Additional guidelines for various types of leaf objects are given at the end of this appendix.)

- Each object name must be unique in the container where the object is located. For example, you can't have two different OUs named Sales located under the same Organization container. Neither can you have two users with the same name in the same container. For example, users Ken Neff and Kalene Neff cannot both have the username KNEFF in the same container. However, you could have User object Ken Neff residing in the Cody container and User object Kalene Neff residing in the Phoenix container. Since these two objects have different Directory contexts, they could both have the username KNEFF. Ken Neff's context would be:

```
CN=KNEFF.OU=CODY.O=WIDGETCO
```

while Kalene Neff's context would be:

```
CN=KNEFF.OU=PHOENIX.O=WIDGETCO
```

Thus each would be a valid object name as they are unique to their specific Directory contexts.

Case sensitivity

NDS container object names are displayed in the same combination of uppercase and lowercase letters as you originally enter them. However, the names are not case sensitive as far as the NetWare operating system is concerned. For example, NetWare sees APL_ACCOUNTING as the same leaf object as APL_Accounting or apl_accounting.

Use of special characters

You can use underscores and spaces in NDS object names. These characters are displayed however you enter them when you create the object, but the operating system interprets them as being the same. In other words, the container names SALES_SW and SALES SW are seen as being the same. If all of your object names are distinct and dissimilar, this is not a problem.

Every time you need to type an object name that includes a space in a command line, you must put quote marks around the name to avoid confusion. For example, CX OU = "SALES SW". O = WID-GETCO.

Non alphanumeric characters can also be used in object names. However, if the object will be accessed from a non-NetWare 4 client (such as a bindery-based client), certain restrictions apply.

Restrictions when using bindery emulation

Whenever you create NDS container objects that will be accessed from bindery-based clients through bindery emulation, the names must adhere to the following rules in order to make them accessible by the non-NDS client:

- Non-NDS clients can only "see" the first 47 characters of any object's name. Thus if the object name is longer than 47 characters, the non-NDS client cannot see the whole name.

- Spaces in container object names are replaced by underscores when seen by the non-NDS clients.

- The following special characters are not allowed in container names that must be accessed by non-NDS clients:

  /   (Slash)

  \   (Backslash)

  :   (Colon)

  ,   (Comma)

  *   (Asterisk)

  ?   (Question mark)

  ;   (Semicolon)

All other special characters are recognized, but not recommended, as they can add unnecessary complexity for your users.

I recommend avoiding special characters in object names even when you are not using bindery emulation. Doing so reduces unnecessary complexity for your users.

T I P

If you have a need for managing objects that are created using different code pages (such as on a worldwide network), use only characters that are common to all of the code pages you will be using. This ensures you can see the correct names of all of your container and leaf objects.

Naming Other NDS Objects

For other NDS objects, such as printers, modems, and workstations, I recommend you decide on and implement a relatively easy naming scheme that provides recognizable identification for these objects. This will enhance Directory search capabilities for your users and help make access to network resources easier and quicker.

Use the naming suggestions to set up similar naming conventions for all shared resources on your network, according to your specific needs. Following is a list of possible naming conventions you could use for common network resources:

`APL_`	Apple LaserWriter printer
`HPL_`	Hewlett-Packard LaserJet printer
`CPMQ_`	Compaq PageMarq printer
`PLOT_`	Plotter
`NPS_`	NetWare print server

287

```
NPQ_          NetWare print queue

HM_           Hayes modem

HCM_          Hayes-compatible modem

CPQ_          Compaq workstation

PS2_          IBM PS/2 workstation
```

Remember, these are just prefixes. You should add a specific name, location, or identifier after the underscore (_) to make it easier for users to identify the specific resource they need. For example, you might use

```
APL_Ed's Desk
```

to denote an Apple LaserWriter printer that is physically located near Ed's desk.

These are examples of simple, yet descriptive methods you can use to make resource searches and access easier for your users. While you are not limited to naming your network resources in this manner, try to keep the naming conventions as simple as possible and make them consistent across the network. This ensures your users can easily recognize and use the proper network resources.

No matter how you decide to name your network resources, be sure to document the naming conventions and provide a written copy of your naming convention standards to all of your network administrators. This ensures consistency and ease of use across the entire network.

Sources of Additional Help

A number of sources are available for additional NetWare education and technical support. Novell provides a number of programs and services to help network administrators and users. Third-party vendors also supply help and training for NetWare-based systems.

This appendix lists some of the main sources of help you may want to consider. While this list is not exhaustive, it does provide a good sampling of the types of help that are available.

Novell Programs and Services

Novell recently consolidated access to all of its service programs into a single toll-free phone number: 800-NETWARE (800-638-9273). This toll-free number is accessible only from the United States and Canada. From all other locations, call 801-429-5588.

Novell's NetWire

One of the most popular sources of NetWare support are Novell's online NetWire forums available through the CompuServe Information Service. Through NetWire, users can submit questions to Novell technicians and share technical information and ideas with other non-Novell system administrators. NetWire also contains lists of NetWare-compatible products and includes files from Novell that users can download. NetWire has a special NetWare 4 forum (NETW4X), with a section dedicated to NetWare Directory Services.

To access NetWire on CompuServe, you'll need a CompuServe subscription, a modem, a communications program, and a workstation. Members of CompuServe can access NetWire by simply accessing CompuServe and typing **GO NETWIRE** at the ! prompt. To go directly to the NetWare 4 section of NetWire, type **GO NETW4X** at any CompuServe ! prompt.

If you're not yet a member of CompuServe, a free trial membership, with $15 of usage credit, is available to let you examine the NetWire service. You can get more information by calling CompuServe at 800-524-3388 in the U.S. and Canada, or 614-457-0802 outside the United States, and asking for Representative #200.

Novell Application Notes

Another service Novell provides is *Novell Application Notes* (formerly *NetWare Application Notes*). This monthly technical publication provides in-depth information about designing, managing, and optimizing Novell networks. It covers NetWare, UnixWare, and other Novell products.

To subscribe to the AppNotes, call the following numbers:

- Inside United States: 800-377-4136

- Outside United States: 303-297-2725

If you mention this book and give the Pcode GBHBOOK when you order, you can get a discount on a one-year subscription to *Novell Application Notes*.

Network Support Encyclopedia

The Network Support Encyclopedia (NSE) is an electronic infobase containing a collection of network technical information on CD-ROM. The NSE provides a single source of network technical information collected from Novell and third parties, including Novell FYIs and technical bulletins; Novell product documentation; the NetWare Buyer's Guide; Novell press releases; additional product information; downloadable NetWare patches, fixes, device drivers, and utilities; and diagnostic decision trees.

Novell technical support

To provide technical support and service as quickly and efficiently as possible, Novell relies heavily on third-party service partners. Novell and its service partners offer customers several options for support.

- Local Novell Authorized Resellers are encouraged to provide product service and support directly to their customers. Many resellers have qualified technicians on staff to handle users' technical support needs.

291

- The Novell Authorized Service Center (NASC) program identifies service centers worldwide that have been designated by Novell as specialists in providing NetWare service.

- Novell offers several options for direct telephone support.

For more information about Novell's technical support programs or to receive a current list of NASCs, call 800-NETWARE.

Novell education programs

Novell also provides advanced NetWare training for on-site support personnel through its education programs. These programs and products are designed to help people develop the skills needed to use, manage, and support Novell's products and networking technologies effectively.

Novell Education has developed a number of NetWare 4-related courses. These are taught by Certified NetWare Instructors (CNIs) and are available worldwide through more than 900 Novell Authorized Education Centers (NAECs) and Novell Education Academic Partners (NEAPs). Novell also offers independent, self-paced study through a variety of computer-based training (CBT) products.

Within Novell's education programs are the Certified NetWare Engineer (CNE) and Enterprise CNE (ECNE) programs designed to provide resellers, independent service providers, and user technicians with advanced NetWare training. Novell has also developed the Certified NetWare Administrator (CNA) program for users who handle day-to-day network management tasks. A person who certifies through any of these programs is recognized by others in the network computing industry as a competent, knowledgeable resource for network management and support. Candidates become certified by passing a test or series of tests.

For more information about Novell Education courses, products, and certification programs, call 800 233-EDUC (800-233-3382) in the United States and Canada. In all other locations, call 801-429-5508.

Publications

Almost all trade magazines that deal with the personal computing industry cover networking issues to some degree. Here are some useful magazines that can provide more specific information about networks, NetWare 4, and related subjects.

- *NetWare Connection*
  Published bimonthly by NetWare Users International
  NUI is a Novell-sponsored organization that offers users the opportunity to communicate among themselves and with Novell. NUI members receive the bimonthly magazine free. For more information about NUI, call 800-NETWARE in the United States, or fax a request for information to 801-429-3905.

- *LAN Magazine*
  Published by Miller Freeman
  600 Harrison Street
  San Francisco, CA 94107
  800 234-9573
  303 447-9330

- *LAN Times* and *NetWare Technical Journal*
  Published by McGraw-Hill
  1900 O'Farrell St.
  Suite 200
  San Mateo, CA 94403
  415 513-6800

- *Network Computing*
  Published by CMP Publications, Inc.
  600 Community Drive
  Manhasset, NY 11030
  516 562-5071

- *Network World*
  Published by International Data Group
  161 Worcester Road
  Framingham, MA 01701
  508 875-6400

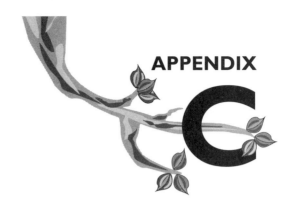

NetWare 4 Installation Worksheets

The worksheets provided in this appendix will help you record the information you need when installing NetWare 4 servers. These worksheets can serve as pre-installation planning tools to help you see what decisions you need to make regarding how a particular server fits in to the NetWare Directory Services tree. You can also use them to gather and identify board settings and driver information for any network boards, disk controllers, video adapters, and CD-ROM devices attached to the server.

Once the worksheets are filled out, store them in a safe place so you can have a permanent record of each server's installation configuration. This record will prove invaluable if you need to make hardware or software changes to the server later.

These worksheets are reprinted by permission from the April 1993 issue of Novell's *NetWare Application Notes*. You can make photocopies of these pages as needed.

NetWare 4.0 Server Installation Worksheet

Server Name: _____   IPX internal network number: _____

Directory Services Context: _____

Hardware/Driver Configuration

RAM: _____ MB   Location of server boot files:
                             ☐ Floppy disk
                             ☐ Hard disk DOS partition   Path: _____

Network Board and Drivers

Name	LAN driver	I/O port	Memory Address	Interrupt (IRQ)	Node Address	Network Address	Frame Type

Disk and Other Boards (SCSI controllers, video adapters, etc.)

Name	Driver (if any)	I/O port	Memory Address	Interrupt (IRQ)	DMA channel	SCSI Address	Other Information

Disks

Drive Make/Model	Size (MB)	Mirrored with disk #	Assigned to Volume (name)

Volume Information

Volume Name	File Compression (ON/OFF)	Block Suballocation (ON/OFF)	Data Migration (ON/OFF)	Name Spaces

Directory Services Configuration

Server Context

O=	
OU=	
Other OUs=	

Administrator Name (for this context): _____
Administrator Password: _____
   (if recorded here, this form should be kept in a secure place)

Partition Management (This information is required only if you want to use a partitioning and replication scheme that differs from NetWare 4.0's default scheme. See "Partition Management Planning" for more information).

Partition name (root container object for this partition):	
Other servers/container objects in this partition	

Locations of replicas of this partition Master replica:	
Read-only replicas:	
Read/Write replicas:	

Time Services Configuration

Time Server Type: ☐ Single Reference   Server Time Zone: _____
                   ☐ Reference
                   ☐ Primary   Daylight savings time observed: YES / NO
                   ☐ Secondary

NLM Configuration

NLM to be installed	Configuration Information

Glossary

Access Control List (ACL)

A property defined for each NDS object that contains a list of trustees of the object and their associated rights. It also stores the Inherited Rights Filter. The use of ACLs should be closely controlled, as the ability to change the ACL is the highest level of rights to any object.

Admin object

A User object created by default during the NetWare 4 installation process. It is initially granted all rights to the entire Directory tree so it can be used to login and administer the rest of the tree. Unlike Supervisor in previous versions of NetWare, the Admin object can be renamed or deleted.

Alias object

A special type of NDS object that is a pointer to a real NDS object. Alias objects allow users to easily access the primary object located in another part of the Directory tree by accessing the Alias object of the primary. The Alias object resides in the same part of the tree as the user needing to access the primary object.

auditing

The process of examining network records to ensure network transactions are accurate and that confidential information is secure. NetWare 4 allows individuals to audit server events and NDS events, independent of the network supervisors (to ensure impartiality).

authentication

A process that verifies that a User object has adequate rights to access network resources and services. Authentication occurs during network login and as a background process when a user attempts to access a new service.

bindery

A flat database that contains definitions for network entities such as users, groups, and workgroups. In versions of NetWare prior to NetWare 4, the bindery provides the capability to design an organized and secure operating environment based on the requirements of each of these entities. See also bindery emulation; Directory Services.

bindery context

The portion of the Directory Services tree at which bindery emulation users can access Directory objects. The bindery context is set at the server.

bindery emulation

A feature of NetWare 4 that allows bindery-based products and clients to coexist with Directory Services objects on the network. With bindery emulation enabled, NDS imitates a flat database structure for objects within a particular container (the bindery context).

Browse

A means of searching for and locating objects in the Directory tree. The NetWare 4 administrative and user utilities contain a Browser function that allows the user to browse through the objects in the tree.

common name (CN)

A naming attribute assigned to NDS leaf objects. The common name is what is displayed in the NetWare 4 administrative utilities to identify the leaf object.

complete name

In NDS, the path from an object to the root of the Directory tree. The complete name of each object in the tree must be unique.

container object

An NDS object that contains (or holds) another NDS object. Container objects organize NDS objects in the NDS tree and help logically partition the Directory tree. Container objects are identified by the naming attributes C (Country), O (Organization), and OU (Organizational Unit). See also leaf object.

context

The location or position of an object within the Directory tree, as identified by the full distinguished name of the object starting with its common name and including all containers up to (but not including) the root.

Country (C)

A type of container object specified in the X.500 Directory Services standard. Use of Country objects is optional; NDS supports it mainly for compatibility with other X.500-based systems that use Country objects.

Directory Map object

An NDS object used to represent a specific file system directory path or file. Using a Directory Map allows users to access a file system directory path (usually to an application) without requiring the user to know the application's or file's exact location on the network.

Directory Services

In NetWare 4, a global, hierarchical database that replaces the flat bindery structure used in previous versions of NetWare. The Directory is a specialized, distributed database designed to enable centralized management of networks of any size. The Directory has a hierarchical, tree-like structure. See also bindery.

directory synchronization

The process whereby all partitions and replicas in the Directory tree are updated with current NDS object information.

Directory tree

The hierarchically-organized structure of all NDS objects on the network. The Directory tree is a globally distributed object database, designed as an inverted tree, with the Root object at the top of the tree and branches (container objects and leaf objects) branching downward from there.

fault tolerance

Protecting a network resource or service against component failure by providing duplicate information at separate locations on the network. In NDS, fault tolerance for the Directory database is provided by adequate replication of the partitions.

fields

In the NDS database, storage spaces that contain values for each NDS object's properties. An NDS property will likely have more than one field to enter values into. For example, the User object's Telephone property might contain fields for the user's office phone number, fax number, and modem number.

Group object

An NDS leaf object that contains a list of User objects to be treated as a collective whole for network administration purposes. A Group object is not a container object.

Inherited Rights Filter (IRF)

The NetWare 4 function that limits the rights that are "inherited" or flow down to objects that reside at lower levels of the Directory tree.

leaf objects

NDS objects that represent actual network resources such as printers, users, modems, computers, servers, and so on. Leaf objects differ from container objects in that leaf objects cannot hold other NDS objects. They are located at the end of a branch in the Directory tree. Leaf objects are designated by the naming attribute CN, for common name. See also container object; common name.

master replica

The main copy of an NDS partition that handles all replica operations. Although many replicas of a Directory partition can exist, each partition has only one master replica. The master replica can be used to create a new partition in the Directory database, or to read and update Directory information, such as when adding or deleting objects.

objects

The basic pieces that define network resources and form the Directory tree structure in NetWare 4. Objects can be logical (such as print queues, groups, and containers), physical (such as computers, printers, and modems), or organizational (such as Organizations or Organizational Units).

object rights

The rights used to control access to an NDS object. These include the Browse, Create, Delete, Rename, and Supervisor rights.

Organization (O)

The container object(s) that reside closest to the [Root] object in the Directory tree. Container objects facilitate organization of the Directory tree. At least one Organization is required in every tree. The Organization container object is usually defined to represent a company, university, or organization that can be further divided into various subgroups. See also Organizational Unit.

Organizational Role object

An NDS leaf object that defines a role or position within an organization that can be filled by different people at different times.

Organizational Unit (OU)

An NDS container object used to represent a division, department, or other segment of an organization. This NDS container object can reside in an Organization container object or in another Organizational Unit container object. See also Organization.

partition

A logical division of the Directory's global database. A partition forms a distinct unit of data in the Directory tree that stores and replicates

Directory information. Each partition consists of at least one container object, all objects subordinate to that container object, and data about those objects. A partition may never overlap another partition, and is named by the highest (root-most) container.

profile object

An NDS leaf object that represents a login script to be executed by a group of users who need to share common login script commands. The users do not have to be located in the same container in the tree.

properties

Categories of information about NDS objects. The NDS object's properties, and the values associated with those properties, contain the information that defines the NDS object.

property rights

Rights that control access to NDS object properties. These include the Compare, Read, Write, Add or Delete Self, and Supervisor rights.

[Public] trustee

A special trustee that can be added to any object. Whatever rights are granted to [Public] are effective for any NDS object that doesn't have any other effective rights. This is similar to granting trustee rights to user Guest or to group Everyone in previous versions of NetWare.

Read Only replica

A partition replica that can be used only to read Directory information. It is updated by information from other servers during replica synchronization. A Read Only replica cannot be used for network login functions, since they require a Read Write replica of the User object.

Read/Write replica

A partition replica that can be used to both read or write (update) Directory information. It has all the functionality of a Master replica except for the replica handling operations.

replica

A copy of a Directory partition that has been placed at another location in the Directory tree. Partition replicas must be stored on several servers in order for the Directory database to be distributed across a network. Replicating partitions eliminates any single point of failure and provides faster access to information for users across WAN links.

[Root] object

The [Root] object is the highest object in the Directory tree. A Directory tree can contain only one [Root] object. This object is created automatically during the NetWare 4 installation process when you create a new Directory tree. [Root] is a placeholder object only; it contains no information.

schema

A set of rules that every object in the Directory database must follow. It includes definitions for the mandatory and optional values of the various classes of objects.

server object

An NDS object that represents a NetWare 4 server installed in the Directory tree. Server objects have special significance because they are used by NDS to track the location of replicas.

subordinate object

Any NDS object that is located within another object.

time stamp

A unique code requested by NDS whenever a Directory event occurs (such an renaming an object or changing a password). The time stamp identifies the event and includes the exact date and time the event occurred. This information ensures that updates to NDS replicas are made in the correct order.

time synchronization

The process used to keep all NetWare 4 servers set to the same time. This is necessary to ensure proper Directory synchronization.

Transaction Tracking System (TTS)

A NetWare feature that protects database applications by backing out incomplete transactions in the event of a network component failure. NDS uses TTS for changes it makes to the Directory database.

typeful or distinguished name

The complete name of an NDS object, including all containers up to (but not including) the [Root], expressed by specifying the type of each object. For example, CN=gherbon.OU=Sales-SW.OU=Sales.=Widgetco is the distinguished name of User object GHerbon in OU Sales-SW, which is in OU Sales, which is in O Widgetco. See also typeless name.

typeless name

The complete name of an NDS object, including all containers up to (but not including) the [Root], expressed without specifying the type of each object. For example, gherbon.sales-sw.sales.widgetco is the typeless name representation of User object GHerbon in OU Sales-SW, which is in OU Sales, which is in O Widgetco. See also typeful or distinguished name.

unknown object

An object that is missing a mandatory property for that type of object. This could result from restoring or repairing an NDS partition. Unknown objects are also created as placeholders during replica operations.

User Template

A special type of User object that contains default information that can be applied to new User objects when they are created. User Templates can be created in Organization or Organizational Unit container objects.

Virtual Loadable Module (VLM)

A modular client program that runs at a DOS workstation to enable communication with a NetWare server.

Volume object

An NDS leaf object that represents a physical volume on the network. A Volume object is created for each of a server's defined volumes when the server is installed into the Directory tree.

X.500

A set of standards proposed by the International Standards Organization (ISO) and the International Telephone and Telegraph Consultive Committee (CCITT) for implementing global directory services.

Index